Wisdom-in-Action

*The Practical Way to be Established
in One's True Being*

Swami Yogeshwarananda

Published by :
Hamsa Publications
34 Castle Lane
Colombo 4
Sri Lanka

Swami Yogeshwarananda is the author of

1. *"The Yoga of Understanding"*
2. *"Divine Virtues"*
3. *"Wholistic View of Life"*
4. *"Mind and the State of No-Mind"*
5. *"Path to Enlightenment"*

Printed at Chandrakanthi Press Int'l (Pvt) Ltd, Sri Lanka.
Tel/Fax : 0094-1-726893 E mail : chan@eureka.lk

Notes to the Reader

1. Whenever a verse is quoted, three presentations are given:
   - sanskrit
   - transliteration
   - translation

2. In the transliteration, wherever double "a" appears, it should be pronounced as the "a" in master. For double "i", pronounce it as "ee" in feel. For double "u", pronounce it as "oo" in boot.

Whenever single quotation marks are used to set off a quotation, this represents a paraphrase of the original dialogue.

ACKNOWLEDGEMENT

It is the patient, untiring, meticulous and dedicated effort on the part of Renee Gluvana in typing the original manuscript, taking out in a disc form and assisting me in editing the book that enabled me to bring the book in print. I thank her, for she has done a great service to the world.

Subject Content

Verse Contents:

12. The natural law of returns.

13. Duty-conscious acquire merit and are absolved of sins. While the selfish absorb sin.

14. The wheel of life.

15. Action performed as *yagna* - i.e. with the spirit of sacrifice - is the basis for the living of life.

16. He who does not follow this "wheel of life" ordained by God, lives a wasted life of sin.

17. The meditative wise are exempted from this "wheel of life".

18. Why? As he has nothing to do or accomplish in the world.

19. Therefore do the ordained work unattached and thereby attain the highest.

20. King Janaka was such an example. Work as an example, for the good of the world.

21. For, the people follow the elders.

22. Lord Krishna is an example, too.

23. If the Lord himself is not a good example, then the Lord himself sets a negative tone.

24. By that the world (people) would perish.

25. Hence the moral necessity of action.

26. The wise should not confuse the unwise.

27. All actions are done by the modes of nature.

28. Hence the wise know the cause of action and permit its flow in their lives.

29. But the unwise are involved with nature and with nature's actions.

30. Hence the Lord reveals the attitude towards action.

31. Actions done with an enlightened attitude frees one from the bondage of action.

32. But the unwise who do not follow the teachings perish.

33. Nevertheless, all are haplessly impelled into action by the impulses of their own nature.

34. Hence one must submit to the good teachings to overcome the natural sensory fascination.

35. To live and die in one's *dharma* is the best.

36. Arjuna asks: What impels man into sinful living?

37. Krishna says: It is desire and anger born of the *rajas* mode of nature.

38. Three examples are mentioned for the covering of good guidance.

39. In life one's good sense of discrimination is always covered by desire.

40. The seat of desire mentioned, so that it can be overcome by appropriate means.

41. When sense organs are initially controlled then one can rise above desire.

42. The practical way to indraw the outbound nature and establish the mind in the Self.

43. Thus to be aware of one's Divine Nature, and be in a meditative state, and thereby overcome desire, which if not, is difficult to overcome. That is through meditation one can overcome desire.

Introduction

The Bhagavad Gita teaches that:

Life is to be lived with wisdom. This wisdom is acquired with knowledge and understanding. Understanding of life brings about a change in vision and perspective. Thereafter with an enlightened vision, one lives life.

In the second chapter Lord Krishna briefly revealed this wisdom-knowledge. This process of arriving at wisdom is taught in the Bhagavad Gita from various standpoints. In the third chapter wisdom-in-action is being explained.

Wisdom is the basis of living of life. Wisdom is also the basis of spiritual life. It is also the basis of all action too. Hence every seeker should seek and acquire wisdom-knowledge. A source for this wisdom is the teachings of Lord Krishna in the Bhagavad Gita.

In it, the goal of life is mentioned. The nature of being of the Divine is explicitly revealed. Nature is explained, what it is, and how it operates and how it functions. Also human nature and how it functions too is mentioned. The problem of human existence with its accompanying causes is well explained. Meditation and how to be established in one's God-nature is practically revealed. The solution to the riddle of life, both in theory and practice is beautifully revealed in the ongoing dialogue teaching.

There are two ways of living life depending on individual aptitude and nature of being. One is involved in action and lives an active life in the world. The other, withdraws from all action, and lives a contemplative indrawn life as a hermit. But for both, one thing is common, that is both have to be established, or rather tend to be established in their true being (and live and function in life.)

The process of being so established is spiritual life. In religious parlance this is mentioned as being God established or living in God, with God Awareness. The whole process is to bring about a shift in awareness. From a human awareness to Self-Awareness. Self Awareness is God-Awareness.

But in the process one has to live life and go through one's actions and functions. Nature within, will impel one either into action or into meditation.

The active (in nature) will be made to work, and the contemplative to meditate. No one can keep quiet. For that is death. It leads to indolence and laziness and makes one unfit for anything.

Through action one attains inner poise. Equipped with inner poise one could effectively meditate. Action done with wisdom promotes inner well-being, and paves the way to be centered, and to be centered in the God (nature) present, within each and every one.

Action should be done for the well being of one, and for the welfare of all. No action is naturally possible only for the contemplative. The contemplative live in God. So should the active. The active gets to God through action. But such action should be done with the "Spirit of Sacrifice". Then such action sanctifies.

But while doing action, one should perceive that all action is done by nature. It is nature which operates everywhere, and impels all action. Hence feel not as the doer of action, but it is nature that is operative everywhere. Thus perform action being centered and detached. When centered one is naturally detached. Thus, even though active, one is calmly detached from action and its results. Action goes on, but the doer is poised in his Self-being. Thus is established in his center. His center of course is his God center within. Thus being God-centered, God experience will transpire within. With it Self-recovery and well beingness takes place and the purpose of life is over.

But in the meantime, as desires overwhelm one, the "way" to get over desires is to get established in the Self.

Spiritual life is the process of Self-recovery. Each one is searching, but knows not, nor comprehends what he is seeking. Nor knows the way to seek. What is being sought is yet to be precisely defined.

The irony is, the seeker is the sought. The seeker is essentially seeking his own well-beingness and a state of total peace, tranquility and inner happiness. To be ever free and joyous is a constant longing in the heart of man.

This wondrous state of existence gets realized when one gets established in one's true being. This truth is the sum essence of the Gita.

Verses 1 - 3

The Bhagavad Gita gives a teaching on the understanding and the living of life. It is not a teaching which logically works out any philosophical system of thought, or even promotes a school of thinking, but in a very brief and terse manner, brings out certain fundamental truths of life. That is all that is intended by it. In the process, an understanding unfolds in the mind of man and he begins to have a clear, or if not, a better vision of life.

Arjuna was having some serious problems about life and the living of it. He was in a crisis, the crisis of not knowing how to go about living and functioning further in life. A serious situation had risen which was threatening his basic and fundamental values of life. Therefore in order to resolve them, and give him an enlightened understanding about life and its living, Lord Krishna, the Messiah, was constrained to give him an instruction or a teaching with respect to the fundamental truths of life, so that once again he could re-live life with renewed vigor, enthusiasm, and understanding.

Accordingly, Lord Krishna began the instruction in the second chapter. Though he was clear in his teaching, nevertheless, Arjuna was having problems in fully grasping and understanding. It is natural that it be so. For it takes time to fully ingest the contents and the substance of a sublime teaching, so that its significance can fully dawn in one's mind. Especially so, when the teaching deals with two specific ways of living life, based on, one and the same instruction. Thus there was a confusion, a confusion in understanding, in the mind of Arjuna. Therefore the third chapter is begun in order to clear the confusion in understanding, with respect to the two ways of living life based on wisdom-knowledge. As such the third chapter begins with the doubt of Arjuna, thus creating the setting for further teaching.

Because in the second chapter, Lord Krishna had revealed two ways of spiritual living - two basic ways of living a spiritual life. He had briefly mentioned them. One way is meant for the person who is leading an active life in society, and who wants to live a full and satisfying life in the world. Thus for him, who is an active individual, one way of dynamic living is enjoined in the scriptures. Then for another type of person, who is contemplative by nature and is an introvert, and has the tendency to constantly meditate, and is possessed of the virtue of dispassion, another way of life has also been revealed.

The first way of life is the *praverti marga* - the path of dynamic living - wherein the person lives in the active world, goes through his functions, duties, and social responsibilities and lives life. How to live that life with enlightened understanding is one way of spiritual living, which has been revealed in the scripture. Then the other way of spiritual living is for a person who has got *vairagya*, - a natural state of dispassion, and who hasn't any further desires to fulfill in the world, and furthermore has nothing to achieve or accomplish in the world. For him the *nivriti marga*, the path of detached living, wherein one is withdrawn from all active action and social living in society, is also well mentioned.

These two disciplines or ways of living a spiritual life are meant for the ultimate good of man and are well taught in the second chapter by Lord Krishna. It is with respect to these two "disciplines" that Arjuna's doubt is all about. Because the two disciplines were revealed to him in one and the same instruction, and therefore there is a confusion in the mind of Arjuna as to clearly distinguish the two paths. Because in the Gita, the teachings of the dual paths run concurrently. The reason being, a sound knowledge of both are equally necessary, for the proper performance of one. Therefore it is the one teaching which reveals the two paths or ways of living life with wisdom. Though the two paths are distinct, they are taught together and are seen to run on two parallel lines, in the entire length and breadth of the Gita. However they crisscross each other in the teaching. In one verse you would find Lord Krishna explaining the path of detached awareness of no action, and then in the next verse he would be talking about detached performance of action - *karma yoga*. He would explain that in a few more verses, and then once again revert back to the state of no-action (detached non-performance of action), and then once again get back to the performance of action. So the teaching with respect to the two paths crisscross each other all the time.

As a result, there seems to be an apparent confusion in the mind of Arjuna. But as far as Lord Krishna's teaching is concerned, there is no room left for doubt at all. Even when a teaching is given, initially people do not always comprehend. It takes time to apprehend, digest, and assimilate the substance of a profound teaching. Therefore, from the third to the eighteenth chapter what was previously mentioned in the second chapter, gets further explained and exemplified. That is, it is made more clear, in precise detail, so that whatever doubts which may linger in the mind of Arjuna, get cleared. That is the intention henceforth.

So we find in the third chapter Arjuna begins with a doubt.

****

ज्यायसी चेत्कर्मणस्ते मता बुद्धिर्जनार्दन ।
तत्किं कर्मणि घोरे मां नियोजयसि केशव ॥ १ ॥

Jiyayasi chet karmans te mata buddhir janardana |
Tat kim karmani ghore mam niyojayasi kesava ||

Janardana, if you consider wisdom-knowledge to be superior to

3

action, then why do you enjoin me on a terrible action, Kesava?

(1)

****

It is a dialogue verily between the teacher and the student, between the *guru* and the disciple. All teaching is a dialogue. It is a dialogue on life. And whatever doubts which arise, the disciple clarifies from the *guru*. Questions are asked and the reply is given. The disciple then asks further questions to be further clarified and enlightened. So on and on the dialogue, or rather the teaching, continues. Arjuna begins the third chapter with a question. *"Jayasi chet karmanas te mata buddhir janardana."* 'Oh! Janardana (Krishna), *buddhi* or understanding is superior to *karma* - action, is your view. It is your considered opinion that knowledge and wisdom is superior to action. If that be the case, *"Tat kim karmani gore mam niyojayaci kesava."* Oh Keseva (Krishna) then why do you enjoin me into this terrible action? Why are you impelling me to this terrible action, even though You say that understanding is superior and is better than action. It seems to be incongruous.' That is Arjuna's doubt.

In the second chapter we find Lord Krishna telling Arjuna that *"Durena hi avaram karma buddhi yogat dhananjaya."* That is, action indeed is inferior to *buddhi yoga*, the *yoga* of wisdom. Action is inferior to the *yoga* of understanding. Also Krishna had said, *"Buddhou saranam anvichha."* Seek refuge in wisdom. For *"kripanaha phala hetavaha."* Mean are those who seek the fruits of action. For, those people who perform action motivated by the desire for the fruits, are said to be low-minded. 'Therefore here I am unable to comprehend why you tell me that even though understanding is superior to action, and action is inferior to wisdom, still at the same time you tell me to get into action? I do not follow this,' was the query of Arjuna. But instead, Lord Krishna talked of *buddhi yoga*.

4

For *buddhi yoga* is wisdom-understanding, which is always necessary for any effective course of action. Therefore, once wisdom is acquired then based on that wisdom, one can live and function in life. Otherwise life and actions would be gone through with ignorance. Hence Arjuna's confusion was with respect to his inability to distinguish between actions performed with ignorance, and actions done with wisdom.

Thus the word *buddhi* - wisdom - stands here for two types of understanding. One understanding is with respect to, how to convert *karma* - action, into *karma yoga*. That which converts *karma* into *karma yoga*, the *yoga* of action is only an enlightened understanding. So it is this understanding which transforms *karma* into a spiritual discipline called *karma yoga*, which would release and liberate you from this world. And that which brings it about is only an understanding. So it is the understanding which has the transforming power to convert *karma* - action - into *karma yoga* - the *yoga* of action. Therefore Krishna said wisdom is superior to action, or rather ignorant action.

Then at the same time, he also gave a further teaching as to what the *Atman* is, that is, what the Divine is. For the word *Atman*, refers to one's true being or Self. That understanding too, with reference to one's true nature of being was also necessary. So the word *buddhi*, wisdom, which Krishna had used there, referred to the two types of knowledge which were given to Arjuna. One understanding was with respect to, the conversion of action into a *yoga* of action. And the other understanding was with respect to, how to maintain one's awareness in the *Atman*, which is one's true being, and still keep on living, and functioning in the world.

Therefore you have to first of all know what the words *Brahman* or *Atman* mean and signify. In the Hindu scriptures God-being is usually referred to by the words *Brahman* or *Atman*. The word *Atman* refers to God-beingness with respect to one's true being. While the word *Brahman* signifies God-Beingness directly. Thus the final goal of life is to realize one's true being which is God-being. Thus in order to realize it, one has to maintain one's awareness in one's Divine Nature. Thus the knowledge of *Brahman* is necessary for maintaining God-consciousness. So if you want to maintain God-consciousness, or God-awareness, then for that purpose, the knowledge of God, which is the knowledge of *Brahman*, is necessary. Thus both these knowledges are included in the term *buddhi yoga*.

Therefore Lord Krishna gave the knowledge with respect to *Brahman* which is the *Atman*. The word *Atman* denotes the God-nature inherent in man and all beings. So he gave two types of knowledge. One was, as to how to convert action into a *yoga* of action, for which wisdom is necessary. And then once again, how to keep on performing these actions as *karma yoga* and at the same time maintain God-awareness, for which too, wisdom is necessary. Therefore in order to see that he's established in God-consciousness, this particular understanding, too, was given. So the word *buddhi yoga* therein implies both the knowledges. (More on this later.) In fact, for the effective and right performance of *karma* as *karma yoga*, you require the wisdom of both these understandings. You have to maintain your awareness in God, that is in your God-Nature, and then still keep on functioning in the world, performing activities.

The chapter will gradually unfold as to how to maintain that God-Awareness. The end of the chapter will reveal a remarkable technique, but the technique and the profound state that it implies has very often been overlooked by mankind. Hence, if you comprehend that you have understood the secret of living. In fact there's no mystery about living life and maintaining God-Awareness. Once you have obtained that understanding, then you have penetrated into the mystery of life and living. After that you won't require any further instruction. That is the crux of the whole issue of living life. While maintaining God-awareness, how to keep on functioning in the world is the burning question in the mind of man. "How to go about it," is what every questing man wishes to know.

There are two types of people. One type of person constantly maintains that awareness at all times because he is naturally contemplative. He naturally sits down quietly, does nothing, but maintains that state of meditative awareness. That is, is always God-aware. While the other type of individual has to function in the world, and performs his duties and responsibilities while maintaining God-awareness. Therefore, while maintaining that awareness, he has to go through active life in society. This is the man of the world. But for both, knowledge and wisdom is equally necessary. Hence Lord Krishna's wisdom teaching in the Gita.

Not knowing this, it was perplexing to Arjuna as to why Lord Krishna gave this wisdom teaching with respect to both types of persons. Even though they are meant for two different types of persons, nevertheless, the same knowledge and its understanding is needed for both. The only difference being, one person naturally withdraws from action, while the other is actively involved in action. That is all the difference.

The truth of this was stated by a great sage recently in the twentieth century. He was a very wise man who spoke very little. But whenever he said, it was very meaningful and spoken in measured language. Very often when these wise people talk, there is invariably a depth of meaning. Here too this wise man, had given the very essence of metaphysical knowledge in a nutshell to mankind. It was the very essence of spiritual living. "Your contemplative awareness or rather your ability to maintain God-awareness, is not based on what you do or what you do not do." God-awareness is not based on whether you do action or not. If you have a natural tendency not to do anything, keep quiet, maintaining that awareness. On the other hand, if you are an active person, and have to go about doing things, then go ahead and do all what has to be done. But only see to it that you maintain that awareness. That's the gist of his saying. Here also that is exactly the teaching of the Gita.

Therefore, Arjuna is putting forth a very pertinent doubt. He could not comprehend the distinction of the two ways of living based on the same teaching meant for two different types of persons. But what he did not know was that, the two ways of living life was successive. When one matures and graduates from one, then naturally one gets into the other. Hence a sound knowledge of both are necessary, so that he could live by one which befits his nature and disposition. That was why Krishna asked him to get into action, how-so-ever reluctant he was. It was not a simple action, but a terrible one in which a horrible carnage was going to ensue.

After all what is life? Life is nothing but a series of actions. Just think for yourself. Series of actions and activities go to constitute and make life. That is all that there is to it. In the world you find terrible actions taking place all the time. And life itself is terrible; and actions too are terrible. Just observe outside. You see the insects. The bigger insect pounces upon the little insect. And the bigger animal pounces upon the smaller creature. Thus life goes on and on. And the human creature too, pounces upon one another. Therefore you find terrible actions all over. There is nothing but slaughter and death everywhere. So life is not a pleasant thing after all. It is constituted of terrible actions as well. Everywhere you see - things are born only to die. Even the dog which gives birth to puppies, swallows the first. Even when fishes spawn, a number of little ones are swallowed in. When alligators give birth, many of them are swallowed by lesser creatures all around them. Everywhere we find terrible actions going on. So life is a terrible thing indeed.

That is why the setting for the teaching is in the midst of a war, a battle-field. Life is a constant battle. There is not only a struggle outside, but there is an inner struggle and a battle constantly taking place in the mind of man. Hence, get up and do what needs to be done, which is to engage in this terrible inevitable action of warfare. That is why the great sage Vyasa's son, Suka Maharishi, who was born wise, took his time in being born and was thus delaying his entry into the world. Hence he was asked by his sage father, "Why are you taking your time in coming? Why don't you come out into the world?"

The sage Suka said, "I am afraid to come. It is a terrible world outside."

Here also, Arjuna is asking for advice, and the resulting advice and instruction given is no easy one. It is a terrible advice involving a terrible action. For the situation warrants it so.

Then he follows it with the next verse.

****

व्यामिश्रेणेव वाक्येन बुद्धिं मोहयसीव मे ।
तदेकं वद निश्चित्य येन श्रेयोऽहमाप्नुयाम् ॥ २ ॥

Vyamisreneva vakyana buddhim mohayasiva me |
Tat ekam vada nischitya yena sreyoham apnuyam ||

(You) seem to confuse my intellect with mixed statements.
Of them, tell one definitely, by which I shall obtain the ultimate good. (2)

****

"*Vyamisreneva vakyana*" – 'these mixed statements are confusing and perplexing me. Your teaching or instruction is confusing me with seemingly opposite and conflicting statements, which have different meanings. Thus you seem to confuse my mind. "*Mohayasi iva me buddhim.*" It seems as if my intellect or my understanding is confused. Of course I know very well, Krishna, it is definitely not your intention to confuse me. That's the last thing that you want, because at this point I have surrendered unto you as a disciple for instruction. Therefore, that is not your intention, as you have incarnated here to uplift mankind. Nevertheless, on account of my limited understanding, it seems as if there is a confusion in me. The fault is not yours, but is mine. It seems as if I am a little confused, because of a certain dullness in my understanding. And why is it so? Why is that, there is a seeming lack of comprehension in me? The reason is "*vyamisrenava vakyana.*" You have used words which seem to contain mixed statements. Hence they seem as if not clear. That is why there is a confusion in my mind.'

We find that in the second chapter, Lord Krishna tells him that the *Atman* is unborn, undecaying, and everlasting. It is eternal. It neither does anything nor causes anything to be done. It is not a doer. It cannot be revealed or known by the known means of knowing. Thus in all these ways, he had revealed the nature of the *Atman*, which incidentally is the nature of one's own true state of being.

Then at the same time, he had been telling him, "*Karman eva adhikaras te.*" 'That your right is only for action.' Having told that the *Atman* is actionlessness, that is, it has no action, and no action can taint or touch it. Then at the same time he tells him, 'You are competent only for action. That being the case, if the *Atman* is free of action, and there is no action in the *Atman,* then why should I do action to realize the actionless *Atman*? I may as well keep quiet and try to realize it! But instead, having taught me all about the actionless nature of the *Atman*, then at the same time you tell me to get into action. That's something I can't comprehend.'

10

The reason for this will be mentioned in the fourth verse - the reason why he has to get into action. Thus because of these seemingly conflicting statements, there is a certain amount of confusion in the mind of Arjuna. Therefore he says, "*Ekam vada nischitya.*" 'Having decided, tell me one only. Don't try to tell me both of these disciplines or ways of living. Don't give me a mixed teaching with respect to the two paths.' The path of action and the path of no-action. The path of action is the performance of action as *karma yoga*. And the path of no-action is the discipline of the contemplative or the meditative life. 'So don't tell me about both of them. You yourself decide which of the two is good and applicable for me and that you tell me.' Arjuna is indirectly asking for intellectual laziness, so as not to go through the rigors of inquiry. He wants Lord Krishna to decide which is good for him, even though Lord Krishna had told him the two paths were essentially meant for two different types of people. It is only when the two paths are clearly understood that a person can decide upon one which is suited and applicable to one's nature of being and disposition.

Now if one does not undertake the inquiry personally, then, growth in understanding does not take place. And without proper understanding one cannot effectively perform, function, or do what one has to do. Even if one wants to be a spiritual recluse, he cannot do so without a healthy and a proper understanding of life based on wisdom.

Hence Lord Krishna is trying to instill this wisdom-understanding in the mind of Arjuna, so that he himself could comprehend whether he should actively engage in action in life, or quietly be. Only when Arjuna himself decides, which of the two courses of action is best, would he be able to confidently go through either course of action.

Thus the two disciplines are meant for two different types of people. He had mentioned this in a very brief manner. Nevertheless, because Arjuna is unable to comprehend the gist of it, he's asking Lord Krishna, *"Ekam vada nischitya."* 'Just tell me one which is good for me, that is sufficient. That is all that I need. *"Yena sreyoham apnuyam."* Tell me definitely about one discipline by which I will be able to obtain the ultimate good, which happens to be, to realize the Divine. Therefore do not tell me of both disciplines, just one is sufficient.'

But the thing is this, in order to live by the one, you require the understanding of both. Through the mutual comprehension of both, the discipline which is good for one is discerned or discovered in the teachings. It is that which Arjuna did not understand. Hence, in order to live in the discipline of one, you must know both. That is why in the world very often people come and ask, "Should I renounce or not?" A classic question. "Should I renounce active living in the world or not?" Because he has not understood the true nature of the two disciplines, therefore he is asking that question. If he had understood, then the very question would not arise in his mind. For, if he had understood, then he would know spontaneously for whom what disciplines are applicable. For whom means - who is competent for what discipline, or way of life? If that is understood, then it will be clear to the person who is asking that question. Thereby he won't ask that question at all. Therefore, in order to know what they are, one must have a knowledge of the two.

Furthermore, the knowledge of both are equally necessary in order to be established in *karma yoga* itself. *Karma yoga* - the *yoga* of action - is not that simple. It is not so obvious or innocuous. It has enormous metaphysical and spiritual implications. In fact the whole of spiritual life is involved in that. For a householder, or a man of the world, it is the most primary form of spiritual discipline, enjoined in the scriptures. If a householder is not a *karma yogi*, he has missed

12

the primary part of his spiritual discipline. Everything else comes within that, as *karma yoga* is a complete discipline in itself. So for it to be a complete or a total discipline, the understanding must be there in total. Then only it becomes complete. Thus has it been taught by the good Lord.

Therefore, according to the question, Lord Krishna is giving the answer appropriately in the third verse.

****

लोकेऽस्मिन्द्विविधा निष्ठा पुरा प्रोक्ता मयानघ ।
ज्ञानयोगेन सांख्यानां कर्मयोगेन योगिनाम् ॥ ३ ॥

Sri Bhagavan uvaca: The Lord said:
Loke asmin dvividha nista pura prokta mayanaga |
Gnana yogena sankhyanam karma yogena yoginam ||

Oh! sinless, in this world two disciplines were said by me in ancient times.
(They were) the *gnana yoga* of the *sankhyas* and *karma yoga* of the *yogis*.   (3)
****

Krishna is first of all inspiring Arjuna and trying to instill confidence in him by addressing him as *"Anaga."* "Oh! sinless." He's referring to Arjuna as sinless. "Oh! pure one." So when he refers to him as a pure soul, he means: Don't worry, you are still capable of understanding. Because that which prevents one from comprehending is the impurity of the heart and the mind. When there is an impurity in one's nature, then the mind is said to be gross. And when the mind is gross, the inability to understand and live by the higher truths of life will always be there. Therefore, he's implying that you're certainly capable of living this life of wisdom-understanding. Therefore, *"Loke asmin,"* in this world - *"dwivitha nista pura proktha maya.*" 'In times gone by, two types of disciplines were revealed by me. Two types, not three, four, or five. Only two types of specific disciplines: the *pravirti marga* and the *nivriti marga.* The path of action, and the path of no-action. The path of no-action is the path of detached living as a *sannyasi,* a hermit-monk, while the path of action is the active life in the world. These are the two primary ways of spiritual living, which have been enjoined for mankind, and have been revealed by me in the beginning of creation. Soon after creation, when man was ready for this teaching, it was given to him by me.' Lord Krishna is not now talking as Mr. Krishna, the son of Devaki. But is now identifying himself as the Messiah incarnate in the world. He is identifying himself here in the majesty and the glory of his own being, as the incarnate of the Creator Himself.

From that standpoint, from his Divine standpoint, he's saying: I have created this universe, and thereafter have revealed the teachings for the good of mankind. In the beginning it was revealed to the sages, so that the teaching could continue in the line of teachers, one succeeding the other. Thus the teachings concerning the two paths were initially revealed by me. Herein with full authority he's revealing himself as Krishna, the Messiah. Not as the mere son of Devaki, but as Krishna Paramatma - the Divine.

He says: I have revealed these two paths. Why only two paths? Simple. It is so obvious. Because you always find these two types of people in the world. Not only today, but even in the olden days, too, you always found these two types of people. The person who is active in the world, and the person who is detached from the world. The latter is a pure soul and has become contemplative and meditative in nature. So all through human society you have found these two types of men. Therefore corresponding to these two types of spiritual seekers, you require two distinct or two different types of

14

disciplines, meant for each one.

And both of these disciplines were revealed in days gone by, specifically for these two types of people. For the contemplative, a contemplative and meditative discipline was taught which is the *Jnana Yoga* of the *Sankhayas*. "*Jnana yogena sankhyanam.*" That is "*gnanam eva yoga.*" Wisdom itself is *yoga*. *Jnana yoga* is the wisdom-knowledge pertaining to the Divine. And the Divine is designated in the Hindu tradition as *Brahman*. Herein the individual understands that he, in his true nature of being, is verily *Brahman* indeed. And having understood this, he maintains that wisdom awareness, or meditative awareness, at all times. He has nothing else to do. He is that person who has obtained total *vairagya* or dispassion. He has no further duties and no further responsibilities, whatsoever. Thus he has nothing further to do in the world, because the tendency to do is not there in him. For such a person who has this natural dispassion and detachment along with a contemplative mind, the path of jnana yoga, or wisdom-knowledge is enjoined. This is an exclusive knowledge-discipline, "*jnana nista,*" in order to be established in one's Divine nature.

This particular knowledge discipline is constituted of three parts. Knowledge discipline is the way of life meant for a person who is detached from active life in the world. His discipline would be broadly classified into three factors. Firstly, all that he has to do is open and expose his mind, to the new teaching and its unfolding understanding that *Brahman* -God- alone is. *Brahman* the Divine is the sole reality of life. It is also the reality of one's being. The individual soul is apparent. And one has apparently become identified with this apparent soul. Everyone in truth is none other than *Brahman*. Each one in their real nature is *Brahman* - the Divine. But in their apparent nature is an individual soul. And the apparent nature is only apparent. It is not real. So what is real is only its reality with

15

respect to *Brahman*. And its individuality as an individual soul is only apparent. If your individuality is something real, if your individual soul with which you are now identifying and functioning is something real, then you can't get away from something real. Thank-God it is only apparent! Therefore, you can get away from this apparent individuality of yours, and realize the true glory of your own being as the Divine. This is the knowledge and its ensuing knowledge discipline.

In this discipline, first of all you open your mind and listen to a unique type of knowledge and teaching which is being revealed to you. As you listen, you acquire it. This initial stage requires that you renounce action, get into a retreat center, and quietly listen, opening your mind to the new understanding, that is being unfolded. The teaching reveals that, thou art the Divine in your essential nature of being. Thereafter, having listened to it, you may still have some doubts left.

Is it so? In what manner? Then through mental reflection you clear whatever further doubts that you may have about your Divine nature, and origin of being. Thereafter, once you are fully convinced of the import of the scriptural declaration, and the significance dawns in your mind - "Yes, I am the Divine," - then all that you have to do is maintain your awareness in your Divine-nature.

Thus the third phase of the knowledge-discipline is a meditative state. In this state of being one is totally absorbed or tends to be absorbed in one's God-nature with all one's heart and all one's being. In such a state, one tends to forget the world and remains quiet, being Self-absorbed in one's Divine-nature. It is a continuous meditative state, and therefore in such a state of being, no activity or interaction is possible with the world around.

Thus this way of life and discipline is only possible for recluses who live as hermits. These hermits are the real holy people of the world, ever God and Truth-aware and focussed, leading a quiet life of piety, poverty and goodness in being with no interest in the world around. Thus this knowledge-discipline is only possible for one whose passions have cooled and who is ever calm and serene in nature, and who is at peace with himself.

This knowledge discipline is referred to by the term *jnana yoga* - the *yoga* of wisdom of the *sankhyas*. Here the term *sankhya* does not mean the *sankhya* system of thought systematized by the sage Kapila. But here the word refers to that knowledge system by which that Divine Principle gets to be known. And that knowledge system which goes to reveal the Divine in all its implication is known by the term *Vedanta*. Hence, it is that knowledge which is referred to, here by the word *sankhya*. It is that liberating knowledge which will now go to liberate you. Having understood that you are the Divine, henceforth you maintain your total awareness in your Divine-nature. That is all that you have to do. This is one type of discipline which was revealed. It is specifically meant for a person who has got dispassion and an all-consuming urge to realize the Truth of life.

Then the other type of discipline, or way of life, or spiritual way of living, is said to be "*karma yogena yoginam*," the *karma yoga* of the *yogis*. That is the *yogis* intent on action as a discipline. *Karma* or action itself is said to be a *yoga*, therefore it is called *karma yoga*, the *yoga* of action. *Karma yoga* is the primary spiritual discipline for an active man in the world who is a householder, a man possessed of a family. So if the householders are able to practice *karma yoga*, they are said to be *yogis*, too. It is meant for those people who want to live an active life in society, and have many duties and functions to perform in life, and furthermore have many desires to fulfill too, along with so many wants and needs in life.

In short, he leads a full life, constituted of *dharma*, *artha*, *kama*, and *moksha*. Every householder is entitled to these four: to acquire merit and wealth, and to have desires and a strong longing for enlightenment. *Karma yoga* is that art of living a spiritual life, keeping these four perspectives in view. These are the four things aspired for by man. Why should the householder aspire for *dharma*, or virtue? So that by virtue acquired he can become pure. He also needs wealth to acquire the things to make his life a little more comfortable.

The householder thinks he is more comfortable, the more he has. But the opposite is the case for a renunciate. For the renunciate, the more things he has, the more the encumbrance. Therefore he chooses to get by life with the minimum. But a householder has a house, a wife and a family to take care of, and therefore he has to live accordingly. A contemplative hermit who is a renunciate has none, and therefore has nothing to take care of. Then of course, a normal man in the world has got his normal desires too, which he is eligible to fulfill in the appropriate way. He is eligible to have all the good things of life.

Then the fourth thing he should aspire for, is to get enlightened. That also is a primary perspective and he should never lose focus of that. If that is missed, everything is missed in life. The other three assume a meaning, only when this too is there. The vision towards the Divine is like the mariner's compass. Just as the mariner's compass gives the direction for the ship in the high seas, to be steered, so too also God-vision gives a direction for life to be steered and focused towards God-realization. So once you have got this vision set towards the Divine, and towards enlightenment, then it is that perspective which gives a direction to your living.

Otherwise, your life would be like a ship which is tossed on high seas. That is exactly the case with most of the people in the world. Their life is without an overall direction, without that spiritual perspective. It is the spiritual vision which keeps everything in proper perspective. Then everything in life falls into place. Life and living becomes clear. Otherwise like a ball, people get knocked about. Either they get knocked about by their children or by their wife, or in their offices, or by their husbands, or wherever they are, they get knocked about. Just get knocked and tossed about in the world. So what gives you a direction in life, is the spiritual or God-vision which stabilizes your life. It gives stability to your life, and gives it a direction. Thereby making life and living meaningful.

Of course it is nice to become a millionaire or a president of a firm, but that is only one aspect of life. But to become the king of kings, is to realize your Divine glory. This brings about a total and a comprehensive perspective towards life and living. Once you have got this overall perspective, then life becomes easy to live. Very naturally and effortlessly you can keep on living. And while you are living, you know how you could live and understand all what's happening to you. Everything becomes clear. It is this vision which gives you the rudder of your ship of life.

Therefore, the householder who has got this perspective performs his functions and duties as a *yoga* of action and thereby becomes a *yogi*, which is a very exalted state. Thus, these two disciplines, or ways of living are meant for two different types of persons. They were revealed by the creator who takes care of his creation. It is these two disciplines which will henceforth be elaborated in the subsequent verses, so that you will clearly know what the science of *karma yoga* is, and what wisdom-knowledge is. Also understand why you would require the wisdom-knowledge in order to live in the Divine and perform your action, in such a manner as to convert *karma* into a *yoga* of action. And while converting *karma* -action- into a *yoga* of action, how you moreover would have to maintain that God-awareness as well. How all that could be done, will be gone through in the subsequent verses which follow.

Verses 4 - 6

Even though the basic teaching necessary, was already given in the second chapter of the Gita, nevertheless, it is not always possible to comprehend immediately a sublime teaching and instruction straight away. On account of prior ways of thinking, prior thought patterns and prior notions and ideas of life, along with misconceptions present in minds, it is not always possible to immediately understand a sublime teaching. When a new teaching is given, there is always a resistance to it from old crystallized ideas and notions which were previously acquired. As such, there is always a room or a possibility for miscomprehension. Either it is wrongly comprehended, or not at all well understood. That was the situation here too with Arjuna.

It is *Brahma Vidya*, which is now being given to him - the knowledge of the ultimate reality, the knowledge of the final truth of life. When a man has lived life based on wrong belief-systems, then it takes time to get over those prior understandings, and be prepared to face life with new found insights, and to once again re-educate oneself, and assimilate the new teaching. Thus the teaching has to be given over and over again, so that it gets impressed in the mind of the student. That is part of the art of teaching. You have to keep on impressing what has been taught, repeatedly and often in various ways. The same truth has to be revealed from different standpoints. And the teaching has to be given from different aspects and view-points, too.

Here also the same process is taking place. We find Lord Krishna elucidating the subject-matter from the third to the eighteenth chapter, what he had already given in a nutshell in the second chapter. He is trying to make it clearer from different perspectives. That is why in the end we find Lord Krishna telling Arjuna, 'I have told you what has to be said. Have you comprehended?'

And the classic answer given by Arjuna at that time was, 'Yes, I have understood. All my doubts are now gone.'

And Lord Krishna further tells him, too, 'I have told you what has to be said. Now you go ahead and do whatever you want to do.'

Then Arjuna says, 'Yes, I stick by your instruction. I will do the way you have instructed me to.'

Therefore, till the end of the eighteenth chapter, the instruction was very classic, and beautifully given. Here also we find, in the beginning of the third chapter, Arjuna had a classic doubt with respect to the two ways of living life. Which of the two ways of spiritual living, as just taught, is better than the other. Was it the *pravirti marga*, - the way of living in the world? Or was the *nivriti marga* - the way of withdrawn monastic living - the better?

Even though it had been explained to him, Arjuna was not able to grasp the instruction, on account of a lack of comprehension on his part. Therefore, once again Lord Krishna is making the two ways of living life, namely the two paths, clearer to Arjuna. So we find that in the third verse he says: 'For the good of mankind based on their different character and nature of being, I have revealed two types of disciplines, meant for two different types of individuals. One is the path of meditative awareness for the hermit-monk, who has total dispassion. And the other, the path of action, as *karma yoga*, meant for the active man in society. These were the two types of disciplines, which I had revealed from times gone by.'

This knowledge was initially given to the great sages. From the sages, this tradition of transmitting this sacred knowledge continued. But then, by and by, as time goes on, everything fades away, including the received knowledge. Therefore in the history of mankind, the need soon arises for the re-transmission of this sacred knowledge. And that is exactly what is happening now.

Thus, all types of spiritual disciplines automatically fall within these two categories. If that is the case, where is the room for religious devotion in these two disciplines? For, religions often talk of devotion - *bhakthi*. Of course, devotion is implicit. It is implicit here, because you have to devotedly maintain your awareness in the Divine, both in the practice of the *yoga* of action - *karma yoga*, and also in the state of meditative awareness in the knowledge discipline - *gnanam*. That is devotion indeed, when one devotedly and lovingly pursues the quest for the Divine. When you devotedly pursue the Divine, then you become aware of the Divine. Thus the only way by which you get devoted to the Divine is to be aware of the Divine. When you are aware of the Divine, that is devotion. It is a state of constant remembrance, in which you maintain this constant awareness of the Divine, and still keep on functioning in the world. And when you so develop this capacity, that is said to be *karma yoga*. In *karma yoga*, the God-Awareness that you have makes devotion implicit. A separate worship as such is needless and redundant, and moreover is beside the point, once the proper understanding of God sets in. Till then, so-called devotion based on religious ignorance will continue.

Also while in a state of meditative awareness, God-awareness is naturally and devotedly maintained too. A person who has withdrawn from society, and is living in the hermitages, ashrams, or jungles, has only to constantly maintain his God-awareness at all times. That is the only thing that he has to do. He is a person who has naturally withdrawn from active society and the only occupation that he has, is to maintain that awareness at all times. While the other person, who is living in society, and is going through his daily functions, has to not only try to maintain the awareness, but at the same time, keep on functioning in the world. So this is how he is telling Arjuna

22

to do *karma yoga*, wherein he has to keep on living in the world, and go through his duties and functions, and then at the same time, maintain God-awareness.

Therefore he says, 'These are the two ways of living that I have revealed for the good of mankind.' Thus implying there isn't another way. So Lord Krishna is very clear, there isn't a third way of living. A man cannot afford to live a good life, without the perspective of *moksha*, - enlightenment, or without maintaining the awareness of the Divine. That has to be the *lakshya* or aim in life to live an honorable spiritual life.

In the fourth verse, Lord Krishna reveals a very significant practical truth of life. The *Atman* is actionless, that is, there is no action in the *Atman* as it is ever full and Self-complete. Then why is it that a person living in the world should get into action initially in order to realize it? The reason for this is being given in the fourth verse.

****

न कर्मणामनारंभान्नैष्कर्म्यं पुरुषोऽश्नुते ।
न च संन्यसनादेव सिद्धिं समधिगच्छति ॥ ४ ॥

Na karmanam anarambhath nishkarmiyam purusho asnute |
Na ca sannyasanath eva siddhim samathigacchati ||

Without resorting to action, a person does not attain the actionless state.
By mere renunciation, one does not attain to the state of perfection.

(4)

****

So Lord Krishna says, *Na karmanam anarambhath* - Without taking recourse to action, and performing one's functions, *purusha* - the individual spiritual seeker - who aspires to realize the Divine, will not be able to attain to the state of *nishkarmiyam*, the state of actionlessness. So through action only, will a person be able to get into the state of no action.

Without going through the normal functions and duties, a normal person living in the world, cannot aspire to attain to that wonderful actionlessness state of perfection where-in there is no action. That state of actionlessness is the final state which will eventually be reached by one and all. What happens is, through action you qualify to get into the state of withdrawal from worldly and religious action. Then once you are in a natural state of withdrawal from action, a proficiency to be in a natural state of meditative awareness arises. This is the state of *jnana nista*, or the state wherein you are totally absorbed in Divine awareness. This is wherein you are totally in a meditative state. When you are totally involved or absorbed in a meditative state, actions automatically drop away from you. Thereafter what happens is, you get more and more established in your God-state of being. Then one fine day, you experience the Divine, or rather your Divine Nature of being.

But where do actions spring from? Actions always arise from a sense of want and inadequacy. You feel that in your human beingness you are inadequate. You feel that you are incomplete, even though in your essential Divine nature, you are Self-complete. In your essential nature, every one is the Divine. That is the teaching of all scriptures: that you are the Divine in your essential nature. But unfortunately, there has been an error. You have forgotten your Divinity. That is the Great Fall. The Great Fall as is said in the Biblical tradition is only that, which means that you have lost your true identity.

Now how did you lose your true identity as the Divine? You lost it, due to ignorance. All that you know is, all of a sudden you

24

found yourself being aware of yourself as a human. This is a self-evident fact, and this is the beginning of your so-called human existence. This ignorance, too, is a self-evident fact or a reality. The fact is you have forgotten yourself, and in life you are constantly searching for your identity. This too, is a fact. So when you forget, that is ignorance. When you regain the knowledge, that is wisdom and enlightenment. Therefore, the truth of the matter is you have become ignorant of yourself.

Therefore, there is a need for the instruction, a need for the scripture to come and reveal to you. 'Look here dear child, you are not a human being. You are not this human individual as you think. You in your essential nature are the Divine itself.' That is why the scripture is there, to give you this instruction - that you are the Divine. You have lost this knowledge. You have forgotten it, on account of ignorance.

Once the ignorance comes in, then the next thing which happens is, you find yourself encased in a human body, with a human mind. Thereafter you automatically feel that you are a human. This is the false identification. You have now identified with your human body and mind. If you have a man's body, you naturally think, act, and behave like a man, and if you have a woman's body, similarly you act, behave and think like a woman. This is all due to the identification, which has now given you a false identity.

But you take this identity for granted, until you are made wise to this natural error. That which enlightens you, and makes you wise is the scripture; the scriptural revelation. It is that teaching which is now taking place. On account of this ignorance, Arjuna is having his illusions of life, and is raving in his delusion. For such a one, Lord Krishna is giving the teaching to make him realize his true identity, and to enable him to henceforth function and live life based on his true identity. Thus in due course, he would realize and experience his true state of being as the Divine.

Furthermore, as the senses are implanted in the body, through the senses you become aware of the world around you. You also become aware of yourself as a human being on account of a human body and a mind. Thus feeling that you are a human being, you feel that you are incomplete and inadequate. Then what do you do? The moment you feel that you are incomplete and inadequate, you naturally entertain thoughts and desires to complete yourself. By merely entertaining thoughts and desires, or by mere thinking, completion does not take place. You have to translate these thoughts and desires into action and activity. Thus this is how you get involved in action. Hence you discover the cause of action. Actions spring from thoughts and desires, which in turn spring from ignorance - ignorance of one's true Divine being, which is full and complete.

So ignorance leads to thoughts and desires which in turn lead to action. Thus the origin of action is discovered. These three are called the knots of the heart, which bind you to this world. Because of the presence of *avidya, kama, karma*: ignorance, desire, and action, you are now prompted into action. And you keep on going about in the world in your various activities. This is self-evident to every one. You feel a certain want in you, and then you want to fulfill that want. In order to fulfill that want, you get into activity. Thus we find one condition leading to another. Ignorance leading to total activity.

Thus, the actionless state of being is only possible when there are no desires. A desireless state is brought about by dispassion, wherein the passions of life have cooled off. When this wondrous state takes place, then one naturally abides in an actionless state. The actionless state goes along with a desireless state of being. In the desireless state, there is an inward tranquillity and peace. The inward peace enables one to become aware of one's Divine nature;

to be inwardly aware, not of the things of the world, but of one's true being.

So when you are free of action, desire, and thought, there arises a tranquil actionless, desireless, thoughtless state of choiceless awareness. This state of Self-awareness leads to enlightenment. The state of enlightenment is called God-realization or Self-realization, or whatever word you may want to use. When religions talk of God-realization, what that tantamount to is a state free of action. It is an actionless, desireless state of God-beingness. Desires and thoughts go together. So it is a thoughtless, desireless, and actionless state of being. What a wonderful state to be in. A state wherein you are at total peace with yourself. And this is what is said to be Moksha, or enlightenment. Therefore, in order to attain to this state, you have to initially go through action.

The next question is, how is it so? How is it that through action, you will be able attain to this state eventually? The reason is, already you are functioning in the world with an ego, or with ego-centered desire patterns. These desire-patterns are the effects of tendencies. The tendencies are the outcome of impressions of life. Thus you have your *vasanas* - impressions, and as a result of this, a certain strong impulse is ingrained in you. These impulses which are very strongly ingrained, have a natural tendency to be expressed, and are awaiting expression. It is these impulses which manifest in the form of desire patterns, awaiting translation into action. Hence to flow into action is a natural process.

You have lived many lives, and in all those lives lived before, you have accumulated and acquired these impressions and impulses which are now within. As a result of these impulses, desire patterns, and impressions, there is a natural impulse within to function and express yourself. This is the psychological aspect of human functioning.

Then the other aspect is; on account of the fact that you have lived many lives before, and done many activities, you have thereby acquired *karma* as a result. Then naturally the momentum of all that *karma* must come out. So the cause and effect of that momentum of actions, or the law of action and reaction, must get worked out. As a result, those actions which you had done before, must find their own expressions in this life and lives hereafter. But only a certain section gets expressed in this life. That small expression of *karmas* - actions which are to be expressed in this life, is said to be *prarabda karma*, or your destiny of life. Destiny means the series of life actions and experiences which you are supposed to experience and go through in this life.

In this life itself, from the moment you are born till you die, there is the series of actions and life experiences that you have to go through, every moment of your life every day. This is the result or effect of factors involved in your previous lives, and they are finding their natural expression in this life. The momentum had already been set. It is like a motor car which was running at 60 mph, and you switch off the engine, and still the car keeps on running till it exhausts its momentum. So here also in this life, you are living out the momentum which has already been set for you. This momentum is finding its daily expression in your life.

You keep on experiencing the momentum of life experiences and actions which has been set for you in this life, with your ingrained psychological impressions. With the help of these impressions - *vasanas*, which are there within you, you are experiencing life. When you keep on experiencing this life, and thus experience out your present momentum of actions, which is your present *karma*, then you are also exhausting these ingrained impulses.

Now the art of living is to live as a wise man. But what happens is, while you are exhausting your acquired momentum in this life, you are acquiring fresh impulses. The ignorant man, who is not well-versed in the wisdom of the scriptures, while experiencing or exhausting out his own present momentum in this life, is acquiring new impulses and setting in motion a new momentum a new series of *karmas*. Unwittingly, out of his ignorance, he is acquiring new impulses and giving his life a new momentum while living out his present life. Then what happens is, this momentum which he is acquiring in this life, along with the new impressions which he is psychologically acquiring, get carried over in the next life. And in the next life, he repeats the same mistake, and thus on and on he goes. This is called the *samsara chakra*, the wheel of life or empirical existence in the universe.

This is quite a how-do-you-do indeed. Then what should you do? First of all you must realize the very futility of this, and put a stop to it. Put a stop to this *samsara chakra* - wheel of life - itself. Therefore, the art of living is to terminate, and exhaust the present impulse and momentum, with which you have come into this world. That is to experience out all the *karmas*, which are meant to be experienced by you in this life, and at the same time, have the wisdom, the knowledge, and the understanding, to see that you do not acquire a new impulse, and generate a new momentum for your next life. What has already been done, let it get exhausted. This is how a wise man should live.

Thus when you are so able to exhaust your present momentum, and have the wisdom to see that you do not acquire a new momentum, still one more factor has to be taken care of. There are still latent impressions in the mind, and karmas awaiting fruition in lives hereafter. They too should be totally annihilated. They are dormant, and awaiting fruition like being kept in a storehouse for the future. All your *karmic* momentum is not to be worked out in this life, only a small quota. The balance which is there within you, has to

29

be totally destroyed by the power of meditation, which you are now going to undertake in this life. As a result, the old momentum for this life gets experienced or worked out, and in the process no new momentum is being acquired, and at the same time, the old tendencies and the vasanas which are lying dormant in the subconscious of your mind are nullified, or burnt away by the fire of meditation. So the fire of knowledge and wisdom, burns away all other mental impurities and *vasanas* - impressions - and tendencies in the mind. Thereafter what happens is, you automatically gain the state of actionlessness. It comes to you naturally. Therefore, you have to get into action, and through action have to now purify yourself by exhausting all the tendencies and impulses.

Furthermore, these actions are to be done as a spiritual discipline, in the form of a *yoga* of action, wherein action is transformed as a *yoga*. This is called *karma yoga*. In *karma yoga* you are to go through life and perform your functions being intent on what you are supposed to do. Without being unduly concerned with the fruits of actions, perform action. By doing so, your desires also naturally tend to disappear. They begin to disappear because you are now functioning duty-bound in the world, doing what you have to do, without giving undue consideration for the fruits of those actions, as the results have already been ordained by the *karmic* laws of life.

When you are now able to function in this manner, then the desires which are within you, also begin to automatically diminish and disappear. Once they begin to diminish and disappear, you become purified. What makes a man engage in action is desire. Without desire, he tends not to act. Hence when you ask him, "Why don't you do this?" He says, "I don't have a desire to do it." But he has a desire to do something else. But suppose a person has no desire to do anything, and is quite calm and content and happy as he is? Then of course he does nothing, and remains quiet in the actionless state.

Who is a happy man? It is said, the happy man is one man who has no desires. For, the more desires you have, the more you are troubled by those desires. Those desires merely come and disturb you. With regard to this there is a nice story of two good friends, troubled by desires. Both worshipped the gods to fulfill their desires. Being Hindus, they worshipped Lord Vishnu. Duly Lord Vishnu appeared in front of them and asked, "What do you want?" One person immediately drew up a big list, and said, "I have all these desires and I want them fulfilled." But Lord Vishnu knew this man is getting into more trouble. Anyhow he said, "So be it. You will have all what you want in your list. But trouble me not with your desires any more."

The other man was a little sharper. He thought to himself quickly. "Well I have all the desires he has, and even more so." So he told Vishnu, "I have also all the desires that he has in the list, but that is not complete, because the moment I give you my list, another list pops up in my mind, soon after. Hence, kindly give me a state wherein I am free of all desires." "So be it," said Lord Vishnu.

Thus when you are free of all desires, there is a *shanti* - peace - which comes. The *parama shanti*, the supreme peace, only comes after enlightenment. Herein you have no wants, no needs, no desires of any kind. Such a person is one who is living in absolute calmness, and is at total peace with himself. Hence it is the desires which come and drive you nuts. It robs you of your peace. Fulfill one desire, and the next desire comes after that. Thus it goes on. Therefore, this is that sublime state which is totally free of all desires, needs, and wants. The *yoga* of action helps you to attain that.

Therefore, *karma yoga*, which is the *yoga* of action, helps you to overcome your desire patterns. As a result you get purified; and then once you become purified, you'll have a better capacity to maintain the meditative state of Self-awareness.

Now what is that which prevents you from maintaining that awareness? It is your preoccupation with your desires, your preoccupation with your thoughts, and your preoccupation with the world. So much so, that since you are preoccupied with all of these, you are unable to maintain this Divine awareness. Hence, once you have got yourself disentangled with this preoccupation, or occupation with your desires and thought patterns, then you will have a better scope to maintain your awareness in the Divine. Thereafter, by and by you will attain to the state of actionlessness, which is that state of freedom. And you want to be totally free. Thus, this is that blessed state aspired by one and all.

Therefore, through action, you attain to the state of no-action. Hence, without taking recourse to action, a person does not attain to the state of actionlessness. In fact, long ago in the Hindu tradition, Shankara, the great commentator had four disciples. One of his disciples was named Suresvaracharya. Prior to being his disciple, he was known as Mandana Misra, who was a well-known karma kandi, which means a ritualist. The two had great arguments on the respective merits on the performance and the non-performance of rituals, and Mandana Misra, the ritualist, was defeated. Thereafter he relented and accepted that ritualism is not the way, and the way to salvation is only knowledge-discipline. After that he became Shankara's disciple, and followed and lived by his teachings.

Once Shankara wanted a particular book to be written, on *Vedanta*. He entrusted that work to be done by Suresvaracharya, the ex-ritualist. The other three disciples took objection to this, on account of Suresvara's past as a ritualist. Because of that past, he may not do justice to this particular treatise.

Shankara understood this, and told Suresvara that before he wrote this particular treatise on *Vedanta*, in order to satisfy the other three disciplines, he should first write another treatise called

Naiskarmya Siddhi - "The Perfected State of Actionlessness." In that particular treatise, Suresvara indicates, why an individual should go through actions in life, and perform his *karma* and activities. There the reason given is, when a person goes through and performs all his duties and functions in the world, very correctly and in a proper way, such a person acquires virtue and becomes virtuous.

Once virtue or merit comes to him, automatically *papa* – sin, which is the opposite of virtue, diminishes. When you acquire more and more virtue, the sin in you, automatically decreases.

When sin decreases what happens is, you become more and more pure. When you become more and more pure, you become purified in nature. Then what happens is, purity leads to clarity. Purity of mind leads to clarity of perception.

When there is clarity in the mind, that mind will now have the capacity to discriminate between what is absolutely true, and what is apparently false. The mind will have that particular capacity because of its purified nature. In due time, the power of discrimination, or *viveka*, dawns in the mind. *Viveka* is spiritual discrimination: discerning the real from the false. Thus this unique spiritual discernment will come to him.

Along with that, *vairagya* or dispassion, will also transpire because papa, the sin, is decreasing. When sin diminishes, the person becomes a purified soul. This state of affairs, naturally brings about the state of dispassion towards the world. After that, this individual will be able to maintain his awareness in the Divine.

Awareness in the Divine means he will have the capacity to meditate. Everybody cannot meditate. It takes a purified soul to meditate and contemplate on the Divine. That unique meditative capacity will come to a person. Thereafter that person will be established in his meditative state, and eventually realize the Divine.

33

This is the sequence. As such, an individual should go through action. Therefore Lord Krishna says, 'Without getting into action, a person cannot aspire or hope to attain to that state of actionlessness.'

On the other hand, some people may think action is a nuisance. Why not we escape from active life and get into the state of *sannyasa*, which is the retired contemplative life of a recluse. So he says, "*Na ca sannyasanath eva siddhim samathigachhati.*" Not by a mere outward renunciation of action and of life, does a person attain to that final state of perfection. So the person does not attain the state of perfection, only by a mere outward renunciation. That means, a person who is not competent to renounce, or a person who is lazy, or a person who wants to escape from life and its problems should not renounce active life in the world. Arjuna gave an indication earlier to get out of the stress of life.

Because Arjuna threatened, in the second chapter he said, 'It is far better for me to live on alms than to take part in this war.' Thereby he implied that it is far better to live as a *sannyasi* - a hermit-monk. He had precisely done that before; and that too on the mischievous advice of Lord Krishna in order to win his bride. So there too, the person who gave him the advice was Krishna. Krishna had told Arjuna to take the guise of a religious recluse in order to win the hand of his sister. Therefore, he had already got into the "habit." In fact, the only person who is eligible to live on alms is a *sannyasi* - a monk - and this has been a custom all over the world.

Therefore, a person who is not competent for renunciation, should not renounce as he will not be able to be quiet in an actionless state of meditative awareness leading to the state of perfection. Why? Because in the first instance, he will not be capable of maintaining the state of meditative awareness, as he is not competent for it. He still has things to do, duties to perform, and so many things to achieve in the world. Therefore, such a person is not yet ready for it, and as such, cannot maintain the state of meditative awareness totally, at all times.

Then what will he do? He will either become lazy or go about creating work for himself. Because he cannot keep quiet and be contemplative as he is not capable of it. Therefore he will not be able to obtain the benefits of the state of *sannyasa*, as he is not competent.

Then on the other hand, as he has left normal life in active society, he will also not be able to get the benefits of a normal life too. Because living a life in the world and going through that life operations and discharging those functions and duties, this person would otherwise have obtained the requisite mental purification. That benefit too is lost for him, by venturing into a way of life, for which he is not competent.

So he has neither this opportunity of getting himself purified by living in the world, and nor is he capable of living as a *sannyasi* - a spiritual recluse. Therefore, he loses both benefits and deprives himself of the benefits of life.

Now the very crucial question is, when should a person take to the state of *sannyasa*? Only, and only when *dispassion – vairagya,* has come. Enthusiasm alone is not sufficient. You can be enthusiastic, but have you got the competency, the necessary qualification?

What are the necessary qualifications for the state of *sannyasa*? There are certain minimum qualifications. One is, there must be total vairagya - dispassion. This is the foremost. The next factor is, he must have the spiritual power of discernment. A minimum wisdom should be there. He cannot be ignorant of life and try to become a *sannyasi*. Knowledge and understanding of life is needed. All these qualities will be there, only when he has matured. Matured mentally, emotionally, intellectually, and psychologically. The sum total of all these will mature him from life, and enable him to take up the next phase of living life as a hermit-monk in order to get enlightened. Thus wisdom and understanding of life is necessary, along with goodness in being.

Then the necessary virtues also should be there. And what are the virtues? Because the moment you become a *sannyasi*, you are a *sadhu*. *Sadhu* means a noble and a good soul. A friend indeed to one and all in the whole universe. A *sadhu* means a benefactor, a kind and gentle soul incapable of hurting and exploiting anybody, and incapable of doing anything vicious. These are the necessary qualifications. Thus he is a person who is at peace with himself. Such a person could become a *sadhu*, and live as a hermit-monk in the jungles and monasteries. He has no quarrel with anybody. Even if others quarrel with him, he has no quarrel with them. So he is a *sadhu* indeed; a noble soul. Such a person who has these virtues, is now fit and capable of becoming a hermit-monk, a *sannyasi*.

In fact, there is a story with respect to premature withdrawal from active life. There was a certain man who in the midst of his way of living, left everything, and came to live in Rishikesh as a renunciate hermit. In due course he developed some qualities and people sought him for advice. But he himself was dissatisfied, and one day told the truth to another *swami* there, that even though everybody came to him for advice, nevertheless, he was dissatisfied. So he was asked the reason. Then he said, that he had left his family and come, and thereby there was a disquiet in him. That was always in the back of his mind. Then the other sadhu told him, "You go back, discharge and complete your responsibilities and then come back and you will be all right." And that is exactly what he did.

Therefore, here also, when all these virtues are there, and when no further responsibilities are there, then and then only can a

36

person become a renunciate-monk. The truth of this will be known to one, at that time. There will be no doubts there either psychologically or mentally. At that time you will know how to go about life. In fact you cannot deceive two people in the world. One is, you cannot deceive God. The second is, you cannot deceive yourself. However much you try, you cannot deceive yourself. So you know what you really are. So psychologically you know what your frame of mind is, whether you are escaping from duties, functions, and responsibilities, or whether it is laziness, or a genuine quest for truth and God.

Then the foremost virtue is, an all consuming quest or thirst for God and Truth with all one's heart and being. It is an all consuming total aspiration and dedicated living as a contemplative hermit-monk with a single-minded aspiration.

Therefore, only when the necessary qualifications are there within, with respect to renunciation, should one renounce active life. Till then the person should keep on living in the world, and go through his normal functions and duties. That way of life will bless him, and confer competency in due course.

So by a mere outward renunciation, or by merely taking the ochre robe, or withdrawing from active life, one will not attain to that state of perfection, if the inner qualities and qualifications are not there.

In the fifth verse, Lord Krishna is indicating that everyone has to keep on doing actions in the world. For there is something within, which impels each one to action in spite of himself.
****

न हि कश्चित्क्षणमपि जातु तिष्ठत्यकर्मकृत् ।
कार्यते ह्यवशः कर्म सर्वः प्रकृतिजैर्गुणैः ॥५॥

Na hi kaschitkshnamapi jatu thistatyakarmakrith |
Karyate hiyavasaha karma sarvaha prakritijaigunaihi ||

Even for a moment, nobody can keep quiet, without doing any actions.
Helplessly all are drawn into action impelled by the *gunas* of *prakriti*.

(5)

****

Everyone is naturally impelled to do actions in the world, as
there is an energy functioning within each. Because of this energy
within, every person in the world is inexorably impelled to be and to
do whatever he has to do. This energy derives its force from the
various thought patterns and desire patterns inherent in man. All that
energy prompted from within seeks its expression, and therefore,
nobody can keep quiet. Hence everyone is active in the world in
some form or the other.

Even the birds keep on fluttering from morning till evening.
The fishes keep on swimming endlessly going up and down in a tank
or in a river. The birds keep on flying all the time. And of course, all
humans too, are doing something or the other from morning till
evening. All life is busy in its own way.

In the world, there are some people who are busy doing
something. And there are certain other people who are busy doing
nothing. There are people like that too. They have got the unique
capacity to make themselves busy in doing nothing, but they keep on
being busy. That is how people are constantly busy with something
or the other in the world. You ask a man to do something and he
would say, "I have no time!" Either he is being busy with something
or nothing, whatever the case be. This is the natural character of the
world. The reason being there is an energy functioning in man, which
will not allow him to keep quiet.

You take a little kid, you cannot ask a four-year-old kid to sit down and keep quiet. Because the energy of the kid is in his legs, and hence the child wants to run about hither and thither. It just keeps on running all the time. Then when the kid grows its energy travels upwards to the waist, and the young man is now very active. Indeed, he wants to get married. You cannot stop the poor chap from getting married, as the energy is now functioning on that level. Thereafter, when the man becomes old and when all the other senses have failed, there is one sense which is still very active. Indeed, it is difficult to stop an old man from talking, as his energy has traveled to the top and seeks its expression therein.

Thus you find that the energy in a person is constantly moving in this manner. Hence nobody can keep quiet. That's why he says, "*Na hi kaschit jatu thistat akarmakrit.*" Nobody in the world can keep quiet without doing anything. "*Karyate hi hvasaha karma prakriti jai gunaihi.*" Everyone does action helplessly impelled by the modes of nature. Everybody is made to do whatever he has to by the forces inherent in him. Thus everybody is helplessly meant to do whatever he has to.

Now why is it that everybody is doing whatever he has to do? What makes him do that? His own *prakriti*. That is his own nature. There is within man a nature functioning, which makes him do everything. There is a nature within you, because of which, you are what you are and which makes you do whatever you have to do. Now what is this nature? It is constituted of the three *gunas*, or the three modes (of nature). All activity in the world is impelled by the three *gunas* - modes - of your own nature. And you are naturally impelled to do whatever you have to do and be by the three modes of nature.

The three gunas or the modes of nature are *sattwa*, *rajas*, and *tamas*. In every one and in every thing in the whole universe, the three modes are present in varying degrees. Everything, be it an

39

animate or an inanimate thing, is all constituted of the three *gunas*. Your physical body is also constituted of the three *gunas*. So also is your mind constituted of the three *gunas* in a subtle manner. Because your mind is subtle, the three *gunas* constituting your mind are subtle. And as the body is gross, it is made up of the three *gunas* in a gross manner. The three *gunas* are *sattwa*, *rajas*, and *tamas*. *Sattwa* is the mode of serenity. *Rajas* the mode of activity, and *tamas* the mode of inertia.

Sattwa is that mode which promotes in a person calmness, serenity, poise, and peace. That is why when the *sattwa* mode of nature functions in you, you are naturally calm, and serene, and are at peace for the moment with yourself. It is so because *sattwa* mode is now operating in you, and thus you are happy. Thus when the *sattwa* mode comes, that sense of happiness also comes in there, and you are naturally calm and poised.

But then the next moment what happens is, it gets offset by the *rajas* mode, which is the mode of activity. Therefore when the *rajas* mode of nature manifests in your being, then it brings about dynamism, and activity, and propels and impels you to get into action and activity. It is then that you have that dynamic energy to do this and to do that. You don't feel like sitting down quietly. You get up, all of a sudden and do this and that. You also get the extra spurt of energy to do Spring cleaning, and various works around your house, all of a sudden. That extra energy has come into you, and you want to mow the lawn and go out to do something. All of a sudden you feel like springing into action.

It is so because of the *rajas* mode of nature operating in you. Also when there is desire, and when there are acute thoughts, and strong emotions like anger, etc., then also the *rajas* mode is manifest. It is active and dynamic, and makes you so too.

Then there are certain moments when you become very dull,

lethargic, and lazy. You don't feel like doing anything. You are just sluggish. At that moment, the *tamas*, the mode of inertia, which brings about inertia and dullness, has set in. It brings about in you the tendency of not doing what you have to do. At that moment you don't feel like doing anything. It is all due to the settling in of *tamas*, the mode of inertia.

Thus you find these three gunas are operating in each individual and as per the manifestation of *gunas*, a person acts. These three gunas are like three corks which are bobbing up in the water. You can depress two of them and one will manifest. And you release one and another will pop up. So you never know which of the three keeps on manifesting in your nature. Of the three, one will always manifest itself. Whichever manifests, according to that, you are for the time being. If *sattwa*, the serene mode manifests, you are at peace with yourself, you sit down very calmly and are quiet. The moment the *rajas*, the mode of dynamism comes in, immediately you get into activity. And the moment the *tamas*, the mode of inertia comes in to you, you become dull, lethargic, and indolent, perhaps a little sad as well. This is the quality of the mode of inertia. Thus these three qualities keep on changing constantly in an individual. Accordingly you are for the moment. If sattwa is there, you become peaceful. If *rajas* is manifest you become active. And if *tamas* is functioning in you, you become lethargic. So impelled by these gunas a person keeps on functioning in the world.

That is why, when Lord Krishna went to the city of Hastinapura to meet Duryodana and mediate in the conflict and try to persuade him to give at least half the kingdom to the Pandavas, he asked him, 'How is it that you are behaving like this in this manner? You also had the same upbringing, the teaching and the training.' For, both warring groups had the same upbringing. They lived in the same palace, had the same teacher, and were provided the same environment. Hence Krishna asked him, 'Why is it that you are behaving like this?'

Duryodana then gave a very classic reply to that. 'Krishna, don't imagine I do not know what *dharma* is.' (Because he has been given that training and knowledge.) 'I also know what *adharma* is.' That is, he says, he knows what righteousness is, what also is unrighteous. 'What you say is very true. What am I to do? There is something within me which makes me act and behave the way that I'm acting and behaving.' That is the wicked disposition, born of one of the three *gunas*. The *gunas* make a man behave and act the way he has to act and behave in the world. Therefore, Krishna says, 'Nobody can keep quiet.' Everybody has to act in the world in some form or the other. So nobody can keep quiet.

But if perchance, an individual who is supposed to live in the world and perform his duties and functions, gives up his normal duties and functions, either out of laziness or as an escape or even by misplaced enthusiasm, and becomes a *sannyasi*, a renunciate-monk, by mistake, then that person, comes to no good.

****

कर्मेन्द्रियाणि संयम्य य आस्ते मनसा स्मरन् ।
इन्द्रियार्थान् विमूढात्मा मिथ्याचारः स उच्यते ॥ ६ ॥

Karmendriyani sannyasya ya aste manasa smaran |
Indriyarthan vimutatma mithyacaraha sa uchyate ॥

Having renounced the organs of action, he who remains thinking of the objects of the senses is said to be a self-deluded hypocrite. (6)

****

Even though his sense organs of action are inactive, nevertheless, his mind will be very active. He will have many desires, and have a tendency to do many things and accomplish them. Hence his mind will be active, and he will now be building castles in the air. It will be running riot indeed.

Such a person who has unfortunately renounced the active world, in spite of his active worldly nature filled with desires and worldly pursuits, will not be capable of leading a renunciate's life of a monk. He is not capable of leading a contemplative life, maintaining his awareness in the Divine. Hence where may his thoughts be? Only in the things of the world. Therefore such a person who has so unfortunately got away from activities, by restraining his organs of action, will only be thinking of the things of the world.

Such a person is a self-deluded hypocrite. He is self-deluding himself. Because he is not leading a life in the world, and at the same time is thinking of the things of the world. He has become self-deluded because he is undergoing a self-delusion about himself; that he is capable of living a contemplative life of the inner spirit and such a life is good for him. But that is not so. Invariably in the world we see this fallacy time and again, in all religious traditions. Whether it be in the Hindu, the Buddhist, or the Christian tradition, in all of them we find a good influx of spiritually incompetent people getting into the monastic tradition.

I remember very well, once I had a discussion on this subject with a head of an *ashram* of a prestigious religious institution in India. I requested him to send a competent monk to a particular place, who would be useful to the community in the area as they had a huge international organization. He gave me a very classic reply. He said, "We don't have the person. Those who join the *ashrams* nowadays, are either the unfit or the misfits." This speaks volumes.

Therefore, until you are fit to renounce, one should not renounce life in the active world. Because the world is the best training ground. People must realize that. This world in which you are living is the University of Life. Don't imagine that in the university you are getting an education. After your education is over in the university, the real university, the real education is beginning, here in life. This is the University of Life, where all the training comes in. Therefore, you miss this training when you leave this and go away. When you prematurely leave this life, the benefit of this is not acquired by you.

Therefore it is desirable to live in the world, it is a beautiful place to live, and to be trained. There is nothing wrong with the world. Don't forget that. All that you need to know is, how to live in the world. That is the education that you require. That knowledge and understanding is what you need. How to live in the world. That is what is now being taught here in the Bhagavad Gita.

Therefore, by error, if a person gets away from active society in the active world, he will lose the benefit of living here, and at the same time, being unfit, will not derive the benefit of a monastic life. Therefore, Lord Krishna says, such a state of affairs is not at all desirable.

Verses 7 - 11

Lord Krishna was saying that the performance of action is always far superior to a premature withdrawal from activity in the world. Until one becomes competent to totally withdraw from the world, one should live in the world, and go through one's duties and responsibilities and live an active life. At the same time, the performance of action done ignorantly keeps a man permanently in human bondage. Bonded to the action and its accompanying results. Thus bonded to living life, the person keeps on functioning in the world unto eternity.

Also it is inadvisable not to get into action, as an inactive man destroys himself through laziness, indolence, and sloth. If that be the case, how is a person to get into action, and then convert those actions into a *yoga* of action called *karma yoga*? For, the primary spiritual discipline for a man of the world is *karma yoga*.

Therefore, in the next verse, Lord Krishna reveals the art of converting action into a liberating spiritual discipline which would liberate him from living in this world with its accompanying problems of sorrow and toil, and lead him to enlightenment. That technique or method by which one is so able to convert action which binds to an action which liberates, is said to be *karma yoga*.

Hence, He says:

****

यस्त्विन्द्रियाणि मनसा नियम्यारभतेऽर्जुन ।
कर्मेन्द्रियैः कर्मयोगमसक्तः स विशिष्यते ॥ ७ ॥

Yestwiindriyaani manansaa niyamyaarabhater Arjuna |
Karmendriyaihi karmayogamasaktaha sa vishisyate ||

Arjuna, but that person having controlled the senses with the mind, performs *karma yoga* with the organs of action without attachment excels. (7)

****

The word *Tu* in this context implies "in contrast to"; in contrast to one who prematurely retires from life and action, that man who performs action as a *yoga* of action is far better. Of course, it is far better to get into action than to physically keep quiet and permit the mind to get into its fantasies.

Arjuna, that seeker should restrain his senses, with the mind, and get into action. For the senses have to be controlled by the mind.

Thereafter, having controlled the senses with the mind, that person *aarabathe* - begins, or gets into action, with his *karma indriyas* - the organs of action. For action is always to be done with the organs of action and thus he performs the *yoga* of action or *karma yoga*. That is, performs action as *karma yoga*. Thus such a person is said to be *visisyethe* - excellent indeed.

For it is well known that the senses by themselves have no power to function unless they get the direction and the cooperation from the mind. Only with the direction of the mind do the senses get into their respective activities and functions. Therefore, it is necessary that these senses be controlled by the mind apart from the cooperation and direction it gives them. It is known that when one's attention is elsewhere, the sound around is not heard, even though the ears are wide open for hearing. The reason being the mind's attention was elsewhere. Therefore, even for hearing, too, the mind has to be attached to the organ of hearing, then only you hear through the organ of hearing. Thus we find that whenever the mind gets attached to a sense-organ, then at that time, through that particular organ, the sensory input is obtained. When the sense input is received by the mind, then it becomes an impression. These impressions get impressed in the mind, as pleasant, unpleasant, or neutral experiences. Thereafter the mind responds accordingly.

Thus when the word "senses" is used in the text, Lord Krishna refers here to the *jnana indriyas* - the organs of knowledge. The organs of knowledge, are the senses which bring about knowledge of external things. They are five in number; the sense of sight, the sense of hearing, the sense of touch, the sense of taste, and the sense of smell. These five are said to be the organs of knowledge through which information is received from the world. It is through these senses that you get the sense data and thereby acquire all the worldly impressions. With the sense of sight, you receive impressions of the form world. Through the sense of hearing, you receive various sound messages. With the sense of taste, you taste many things. So also with the organ of smell, and with the sense of touch, you are able to have all types of pleasant and unpleasant sensations and to feel, heat and cold. Thus, through these five organs of knowledge, you receive data or information and come in contact with the sense world. It is these sense organs which have to be controlled by the mind, so that one does not get lost in the sense world of sensuous things.

Having controlled these five sense organs, then what should you do? Thereafter, with the help of your organs of action, perform action. The organs of action are also five in number. They are the hands, the feet, the speech, and the organs of reproduction and evacuation. With these five sense organs of action, you get into activity in the world, and perform various actions.

And these actions should be performed as a *yoga* of action, *karma yoga*. All actions should be performed as such. Every action that you do, is an action; it is *karma*. The opening of the eyelids, the

47

closing of them, moving the hands, moving the lips, going for a walk, eating food, seeing with eyes, hearing, everything is an action. Every moment you are going about your daily functions from morning till evening, and these functions are the actions that you naturally do. Thus incessantly you are ever active. Spiritual science is to convert these actions into a *yoga* of action.

You are going to do the same action itself and there is no difference as far as the action is concerned. You are going to live the same life itself. And in that too, there is no difference. Because we find, Lord Krishna made Arjuna do the same action and live the same life from which he was going to recoil and get away from. But with one difference - which makes all the difference in living life.

That which makes all the difference is the mental attitude; and attitude is everything. It is the frame of mind brought about by an enlightening knowledge which induces a new perspective towards life and its living. With an enlightened understanding, you go about your ways and live the same life, and it is this new perspective which makes all the difference. Either you can live in the world with ignorance, or you can live in the same world with wisdom and understanding. It is that wisdom-understanding which is now being given to you. So that, with this wisdom and understanding, you would be able to convert life into a *yoga*, and become a *yogi*, a *karma yogi*. A man of dynamic spiritual action.

Therefore, in order to do that, first of all we must know what exactly is the error or the fault in every action. Whenever an ignorant man of the world gets into action, he commits three types of errors. Because of those three errors, action or *karma* becomes a cause for human bondage. Due to these three errors, you are inviting bondage patterns for yourself unwittingly every moment of your life, as you have understood neither the science of *karma yoga*, nor the science of living.

The first of these errors is: Whenever one gets into action and does whatever function he has to do, first and foremost he gets attached to the fruits or results of these actions. He wants to do an action motivated by the desire to reap the fruits of that action.

If you ask a little boy, perhaps your little son, to go to the nearby store and get something, which is immediately needed in the house, he is reluctant to do so. But, when you tempt and tell him, "Get some sweets as well for yourself," he does it. Thus we see, motivated by the sweets he is now going to do an action which in any case, he should have done.

Similarly also, this is the flaw in the action of man. That little boy has to do that action because he's a member of the family, and therefore he's supposed to do that little function which his mother wanted him to do. Naturally he should do it and with that the matter is over. But instead he does that action motivated by a result. Then with all joy he does it. This is the first error in the performance of action. Motivated by a desire to reap the fruits of action, man performs actions.

The enthusiasm for the fruits of actions becomes so strong, that those results become the motive force and the motive power to propel you into action in the world. What happens by that is, as you are so motivated to get into action, that you will have to reap the fruits of those actions, as well. As you have generated the impulse within you and have created a strong urge to obtain the fruits of those actions.

In case you don't get the fruits of those actions in this life, you are going to get them in your next life. Thus have you generated an impulse within, to prolong your human existence or the agony of your human life. The agony of your human life gets prolonged, and ᴖarried over into the next life, because of this initial error.

Man has to overcome this error of being attached to the results of action. The way to do it is not to be concerned with the results, but to do whatever has to be done. From morning till evening, everyone has got his or her work cut out for the day. These are the obligative functions and duties. As and when they occur each one knows what has to be done. Some of these functions come unexpected, and that too, one knows has to be done. These actions may transpire either in the office or in the home, or in some social context. They are all to be gladly executed and with that the matter is over.

Therefore, whatever functions and duties which come your way in life, have to be willingly and gladly done. It is also quite nice to have unexpected action, otherwise life can be boring. From morning till evening if you exactly and precisely know what to do, life can become unexciting. If an astrologer were to reveal to you every minute of your life, do you think you would want to know it? You'll tell him to give an overall estimate. If not, that would make your life utterly boring. Therefore, in life, many unexpected activities and functions come, and they are all to be done pleasantly and calmly.

Why should you do it? Because it has to be done. That's the only reason. Those actions just come your way. You are placed in a particular situation, and hence you have to do it. Thus you just merely undertake it and perform it. When you so do it, perform it to the best of your ability. Give the best you can on each occasion, as per your ability. That is why one of the definitions for the state of *yoga* is: "*yogaha karmasu kaushalam.*" The meaning is twofold. One is "dexterity in action is *yoga*," and the other is, "efficiency in action is *yoga*." Action in both senses is equally applicable. Everything has to be done efficiently and well. Normally people have a problem in not being focused upon what they are doing. They are not able to dedicatedly apply themselves upon anything. That being the case, *upasana* - or mental acts of religious worship, bring the mind into focus. Thereby the mind acquires the capacity to focus upon whatever being done. As the mind is dissipated, the capacity to be focussed is acquired through *upasana*, or religious worship. Thereafter the mind becomes competent to effectively meditate. The same result can be acquired in the daily actions itself. If you go through actions with complete dedication, and apply your whole mind upon what you are doing, then you develop the same capacity to be focussed. The mind is thus no more dissipated, and is concentrated upon whatever is being done. Thereafter the same focussed mind can be used for meditation. Thus this unique capacity comes as a side result, to one who does actions with all attention.

In the second chapter of the Gita, *yoga* is defined as *"yoga karmasu kausalam."* That is - dexterity in action is *yoga.* Herein dexterity means, having the ability to convert an action, which binds you, into a liberating spiritual discipline. That *yukthi*, or method, or science in action, is said to be *yoga.* An action which would have bound you, is being worked out by you for your own benefit towards liberation. Such a performance of action is said to be dexterity in action, or *yoga.*

The second error is that every person is attached to the very action itself. The first defect is, to be attached to the results or fruits of action. Since you are attached to the very action itself, you say, "I like to do this, I don't like to do that." This is so because one is attached to the action. Thus the question of doing it or not, seems to be based on whether you like to do it or not. This is not the basis for the performance of action. The basis of action is based on the duty and need of it being done. When anything has to be done, you may as well do it with all enthusiasm. As circumstances in any case will impel and compel you into that action. That is why Lord Krishna said in the Gita, 'Even if you do not want to engage here in battle,

Arjuna, you may as well willingly get into the present action awaiting you, as you would be inexorably drawn into it by the force of events.'

It is like getting a little boy, over whom you have authority, to do a piece of action. The boy is reluctant to do it, but nevertheless you make him do it, as he has to do it. So reluctantly, fretting and fuming, he does it, knowing that he has to do it. This is exactly the situation with grown-up people too. Very often, fretting and fuming, they go about doing things, even though knowing very well in their heart that they have to do them. That being the case, why not do it pleasantly and peacefully without the frets and the fumes. This is where responsibility and wisdom comes in. When you shirk your responsibility, you do not want to do it, but when you accept your responsibility, willingly you undertake your functions.

Sometimes more work is thrust upon you, and in such a situation what should you do? Go ahead and do it, because it has come your way. That is why it has come to you. Such a situation is called as "*prabala prarabda.*" A strong and compelling *karma* awaiting execution. It comes to you like a force, as if it is sitting on top of you, making you do it, whether you want to or not. Since it has to be done, go ahead and do it, with a pleasant frame of mind. After all, life itself is constituted of a series of actions. So if you are going to fret and fume with your actions and not go into it with a pleasant frame of mind, you are thereby creating a stress in the flow of your life.

Therefore, in order to live life, in the manner you are supposed to live, you have to maintain your mental poise and equilibrium. That is why another definition of *yoga* states, "*samatvam yoga ucchate.*" That is, the state of mental equipoise is said to be *yoga*. When you go through your functions, and modalities of living life in a serene manner, that is said to be the state of *yoga*. Performing *karma* is living life. Living life means going through various actions and

52

functions. Then at the same time, if you are able to maintain your mental serenity, balance and equipoise, then you are in a state of *yoga*.

But on the other hand if you have this *raga* and *dwesha*, that is - likes and dislikes, and say to yourself, I like this, and hence I am going to do it, and I don't like this action, and therefore I am refraining from doing it, or doing it haphazardly. If perchance you have this attitude, then life has a way of getting to you. Whatever you try to shirk and get away from, will always come back to you in some form or another, in order to be worked out. If it is not to be done today, life will make you do it at another time. So once and for all you may as well as finish it off.

Therefore, the second flaw is attachment to action. Being attached to the very action itself, because of likes and dislikes, a person either tends to do an action or not do it. By that life is going to be governed by likes and dislikes. If it is going to be governed by likes and dislikes from morning till evening, the pendulum of your life is going to swing every moment, because you're going to meet in life many things which you like and also many things which you don't like. So the art is to develop the capacity to deal with both, and be cool and balanced and go through pleasant and unpleasant actions and situations in life. Therefore, get into action, knowing very well that it has to be done, without being attached to the very action itself.

Then, the third defect in action is, every person feels that "he is the doer." If you ask a person who did this, immediately his hands go up to reveal it. He wants to tell the whole world of what he has done. This *ahamkara*, or strong sense of ego makes him feel that he is the doer of actions. If you are the doer, then you shall have to reap its results or consequences later on, as its enjoyer, too. To do this you will have to come back in another life to reap the rewards of what you had done now. Then in the next life too, you repeat the

53

same process, and thus the wheel of your empirical existence in the universe goes on unto time eternity. By this you are unwittingly giving further momentum for the continuance of your existence as a human individual having your ego as the basis. But the idea is that you should realize your Divine beingness and lose your ego-based superficial human nature. Your present human nature is only an apparent phenomenon. Your apparent individuality is all due to your ego. In your real nature, thou art the glorious Divine. Therefore, the third fault in action is the feeling of I.

Therefore, how should you do an action and get over this erroneous notion of oneself? The way to do this is to perform the action in an unassuming manner. In an unassuming manner means, in a natural manner, the action is done. You are only concerned with the action. It's done, and feel to yourself that you are only an instrument.

That is why Lord Krishna said to Arjuna, "*nimitta matram bhava*," 'Become only an instrument. All these people have already been killed by me,' says Lord Krishna, 'don't think you are going to kill them.' Because that is what Arjuna said, 'I shall be killing them.' By that Arjuna strongly feels that he is the doer of an action and therefore he is the killer. But then Lord Krishna says, 'No, I have already killed them.' That is why even before the battle began, Lord Krishna shows the cosmic form, in the *viswaraupa darshana* to Arjuna. In that he is revealing what is going to transpire eighteen days later.

Before the actual war began, on the first day itself, he is showing what finally transpired at the end of the war on the eighteenth day. That is why Lord Krishna says, 'I have brought about all this.' As the creator, protector, and organizer of this universe, the course of things have been schemed and worked out by me. Everything with respect to Arjuna's life has been worked out. Similarly too, it has been worked out for every single person in the whole universe. All that a person has to do is, play his role in life as an instrument as life unfolds itself.

Just as in a theatrical play, every stage-actor has been assigned a role, and accordingly plays his part at the assigned moment to the best of his innate ability, with all earnestness and enthusiasm. Similarly too, in the unfolding of the cosmic drama of life, each human actor has been assigned a lifetime role, and thus all that he has to do is play his duly assigned part, knowing full well that he is only an actor on the real stage of life. If the significance of this dawns in his mind, then he would be able to negotiate the tragedies and comedies of life with a twinkle in his eye. Then life would be a walk-over.

The only difference being, in a theatrical play each actor knows what and when his assigned role is, and thus eagerly awaits his dramatic moment. But on the stage of life, there is a glorious uncertainty, and each human actor is expected to play his part spontaneously, as the occasion and the moment arises, not knowing what his role is, and how the drama of life would unfold, take its due course, and have its end. This is the glorious uncertainty of living life. A little reflection within would reveal that life indeed is a drama. Indeed married life is even more so. It is a glorious soap opera, with all its tears of joy and tears of sorrow.

It is God the creator, who as the cosmic architect, with all cosmic powers, who has planned and worked out in detail the life and all the actions and activities of each and every one in the universe. As such, each one goes through his functions inexorably.

That being the case, then how should one go about life? As actions unfold themselves, accept them as one's destiny of life, and merely execute them as an instrument. Just perform and do whatever has to be done. With that it is over. Thus, it is in this manner that action is converted into a *yoga* of action.

So don't imagine that *karma yoga* means doing social work. No, not at all. In fact, a housewife may never have done any social work in her life, and yet she may be a *karma yogi*. On the other hand, a person all through his life may have been a social worker, but if he had gone through life functioning with an egotistical feeling that I am the doer, and having not understood the science of *karma yoga*, may not be a *karma yogi* at all. So *karma yoga* is not based on what you do, but on how you do, what you have to do. With what attitude you do, what has to be done by you.

So it is this attitude which makes it a *yoga* of action. And this attitude is based on an enlightened understanding. This enlightened understanding is what is called "*Buddhi yoga*." That is why Krishna says, "*Buddhou saranam anvichha*." That is, "May you take refuge in the *yoga* of wisdom-understanding." It is this enlightened understanding which converts action into a *yoga* of action. Of course, social duties are part of one's natural daily duties, and there is no doubt about that. But what makes it into a *karma yoga* is the mental frame with which one functions, being free of the three defects. That is to say, you go through your daily functions without being attached and concerned with the fruits of action; secondly, without being attached to the very action itself. And thirdly, without having the sense of ego-based doership. When these three errors in action are not there, then you are a *karma yogi*. This is how *karma yoga* is to be performed.

But mind you, with this it is not complete. One more factor is needed. That is why Lord Krishna gave the knowledge of the Ultimate Reality (*Brahma jnana*) as well to Arjuna. The Ultimate Reality happens to be the true Self of each one. Thus the knowledge about the *Atman* - the Self, was also given. Why did he give him this knowledge, too, even though he had asked him to get into *karma yoga*? He did this, so that Arjuna could also maintain his awareness in the Divine, which is the true Self of one's being. Because he also wanted him to do that. Then only it becomes *karma yoga*. The idea is, *karma yoga* really becomes complete and meaningful only when the individual seeker, at the same time maintains his awareness in the Divine. Therefore, while going through your functions, your mind should also be established in the Divine.

How does the mind get established in the Divine? A beautiful example given by the saint Ramakrishna will make it very clear. A newly married couple are settled in life after their honeymoon. The young girl is at home, and the young man is at work in the office. The girl is taking care of her house and her household chores. Where do you think the mind of that girl will be while going through her normal functions? It'll be on the young man working in the office. Not that she constantly thinks of him, but certainly her awareness would be on him. And similarly, the poor chap, too, while working in the office, would have his mind on the girl at home. In the same manner for everyone, while working and functioning in the world, one's awareness too, should be in the Divine.

The other example which is so apt is: In Indian villages there is a village life which goes on. Therein the village girls go to the village well to draw water. These girls go as a group. And as a group, they are relaxed and easy-going. As such, being in their natural element, they frolic, laugh, giggle, sing, and do everything. At the same time, they would be having two or three pots balanced on their head, one on top of the other. During this time, they would be singing, walking, talking, cracking jokes, etc. They'll be doing all these functions, but all the while, the periphery of their awareness would be on the balancing of the pots. Just as much as the girl's peripheral awareness would be on the boy, so too also the peripheral awareness of these girls would be on the balancing of the pots. In the same manner, you keep on living life and going through your various functions and at the same time, maintain the peripheral awareness in the Divine.

As to how to do it, we will see subsequently. When that particular verse comes, we will go into that in detail. But now let it suffice that the peripheral awareness should be in the Divine. At the same time go about going through your daily functions, and activities. When you go about your daily functions and activities, that is called living life. Your functions and activities are your life. Thus you're living life and at the same time, are God-conscious.

You see how simple and, yet how profound it is. As you keep on gradually developing this capacity, what was the peripheral God-awareness gradually becomes a natural part of your consciousness. It has become natural to your awareness or part and parcel of your awareness. This has come about effortlessly and naturally in course of time.

Thus God-consciousness is naturally being maintained all the time. Thereafter, as you get more and more absorbed in it, God-awareness becomes more intensified. Thus, gradually, you become so absorbed, that actions begin to naturally drop away from you as you have now become more focussed in your Divine nature. It is now an all-consuming absorption. You are so totally absorbed, that you begin to, not only forget activities, but also begin to lose awareness of the surroundings and of the world, too. At this point the world begins to recede from your consciousness. And finally you become so God-absorbed that the mind has become unaware of anything else. Now the mind could be said to be firmly established in the Divine. At this point all activities naturally drop away. It is the actionless state of being. Thus a person naturally comes to abide in that Blessed state in this manner.

Therefore, the science of *karma yoga* is only made complete if this important factor, namely the mind becoming God-aware, is incorporated in living and pursuing one's life and its actions. Thus maintaining this peripheral God-consciousness, keep on doing all your duties and functions.

The word *asakthaha* here stands for - without being attached to the fruits of action, and also without being attached to the very action itself. When you are able to go through actions in this manner, then it is said to be *karma yoga* or the *yoga* of action. This is a very exalted and desirable spiritual state for aspirants seeking liberation.

Then he says in the next verse:

****

नियतं कुरु कर्म त्वं कर्म ज्यायो ह्यकर्मणः ।
शरीरयात्रापि च ते न प्रसिध्येदकर्मणः ॥ ८ ॥

Niyatam kuru karma tvam karma jiiyo hiykarmanaha |
sareerayaatraapi ca te na prasiddyedakarmanaha ||

May you do the enjoined actions; action is superior to inaction. Even the maintenance of the body is not possible for the one without action. (8)

****

You are enjoined to do your *niyatham karma*, which means obligative duties. You only know, what obligatory functions you have. From morning till evening, whatever duties and functions which you have and which you are supposed to do, is your duty. You are duty-bound to assume the responsibility to perform them. Thus nobody has to tell you what you have to do. You yourself know what needs to be done.

"*Karma jiayo hi akarmananaha.*" Action is superior to inaction. The performance of action is far superior to their non-performance, because the very non-performance of obligative duties brings about many defects. The first defect is, it makes you good for nothing. When you go through life and don't do what you have to do, and shirk away from your functions and activities and refrain from your actions, in course of time, you become lazy, dull, good for nothing and your entire mind and life become disorganized. Prior to that, the mind, which had a capacity of organization, now begins to disintegrate. You as an individual person, begin to disintegrate mentally, as an organized being. Psychologically, all your competency and ability goes away.

It is well known that, when you take a short holiday, even for a few days, it takes one or two days to get back into rhythm. You are a little lazy and lethargic to get back to your normal functions. If you have a big layoff from work, it will take a long time to get back to your normal rhythm. Because what happens is, you have taken life so loosely and easily, that every capacity you have, begins to wither away. That is why the musicians and singers, have to sing every day to keep their vocal cords in good trim. If not, they lose it. To get back to good singing once again takes time. Even in sports, if you keep away from the sport, your ability to function at your best takes time. Thus efficient performance of every action is similarly so, including the living of life, too.

Therefore the premature withdrawal from action and not doing what one is supposed to do, is most undesirable. As such, all the functions you have must be done. Thus whatever work is entrusted to you in your office, you willingly do it. Also whatever duties that you have at home, that also, you willingly do. And whatever social duties you have, that too you do because you are a social being, living in a collective society. Thus, man has essentially three types of duties. The duty in the office, the social duty, and the duty at home. And none of the three should be neglected, as all three are equally important and what's more, related to his daily living. Then only he leads a balanced life with a sense of responsibility. This is said to be *niyatam karma*.

In case you shirk from functioning, even the maintenance of the body is not possible. For one who does not work, even the living of life is not possible. If a man were to think to himself, "Oh, let the goods of my life come to me," do you think it will happen? If a lion were lazy to hunt will the deer enter the mouth of the lion? However mighty the lion is, even if it were a sleeping lion, it too, will have to fend for its food or perish. Therefore, every person has to get into action, as action indeed is far superior to inaction.

Once again, Lord Krishna is bringing out this idea of action and its profound significance from another perspective. From the perspective of *yagna*, or sacrifice, how is a man to live in the world? He now explains the concept of "*yagna*," that is, sacrifice. This sublime idea has been misunderstood and wrongly practiced in India for centuries. This verse opens out its mystic significance:

****

नियतं कुरु कर्म त्वं कर्म ज्यायो ह्यकर्मणः ।
शरीरयात्रापि च ते न प्रसिद्ध्येदकर्मणः ॥ ९ ॥

Yagnaarthatkarmanoanyatra lokoyam karmabandhanaha |
Tatartham karma kaunteya muktasanghaha samaacara ||

This world is bound by action, when action is not done as a sacrifice. (Hence), son of Kunthi, as a sacrifice perform action very well, being free of attachment.   (9)

****

Apart from the performance of action as a "*yagna*" (sacrifice), any other way of performing action, only leads to bondage in action.

The word *yagna* means sacrifice. In its narrow, literal sense, it is well known that *yagnas* are performed by ritualistic priests in a sacrificial altar, and oblations of varied things are offered therein. Such a sacrifice is performed to please the gods, and to live off the innocence of the people. But *yagna* in its true sense has a wider and a deeper application to the living of a good spiritual life of sacrifice. And that is, the very living of one's life is to be gone through as a sacrifice. Whatever works and functions that one does, are to be done as a sacrifice. It is this idea or concept that Lord Krishna is trying to bring out in this and the following six verses. Thus every action in the world, is to be performed as a sacrifice, as an offering. In a sacrifice, there are offerings. Here too, every action in the living of life is to be offered as an offering, as a sacrifice. Then such an action done with a spirit of sacrifice, sanctifies one, and promotes the well-being of one and all. In the performance of work as a "sacrifice," not only is the action done as a sacrifice, but the results too, are offered to the cosmos to be partaken by one and all.

Thus every action that you do is sacred. No matter how simple it is. The housewife who cooks food for the whole family is doing a *yagna*; - she's performing a great sacrifice there. The man who goes to work and toils from morning till evening, to maintain his family, is doing a sacrifice. So any action that you do in the world, is to be done with a spirit of sacrifice. With a spirit of sacrifice, all work done, along with its fruits, is to be offered unto the Lord.

As the scripture is a religious text, it gives a religious example to convey an idea. This example is to be expanded to a more comprehensive meaning indicating that the whole of life, and the very living of life, is to be undertaken with a spirit of sacrifice. Your living of life itself is a sacrifice. So if you can learn to live life in this manner, then every one of you would naturally go through your obligative duties and functions willingly, knowingly, and happily.

But when work or action is done other than with this concept of the spirit of sacrifice, then that work leads one into the bondage of action. Such an action is often done with arrogance, pride, and vanity. This is how the ritualistic priests the world over performed their priestly functions of priest-craft. Such an action leads one into the bondage of action.

On the other hand, if actions are done with this spirit of dedication, then every action that you do is a noble, exalted action. It is in this spirit that Krishna is talking about the performance of action.

Therefore he says, "*Tatartam karma kaunteya mukta sangaha samachara*": "Son of Kunthi, free of attachment, perform action well for that sake." That is, as a sacrifice perform all your actions, being free of the attachment to the actions and its results. Without being concerned of the fruits of action, go about doing all your actions as a series of sacrifices, as dedicated action. When action is done in this manner, then that action is said to be a sacrifice. You don't have to go and perform a so-called ritualistic "sacrifice" as you are already performing a sacrifice every moment of your life. For, every action of yours is now being done as a ritual. Only when you don't understand these principles of life, then are you tempted by the priests who indulge in priest-craft, into a ritualistic sacrifice. But when you understand the true concept of *yagna*, they only will you know that the whole of your life is sacred, and is to be lived as a sacrifice.

This earth plane into which you are born now is said to be a plane of action. It is not a *bhoga bhumi* - sensuous plane. It is not a plane made for your enjoyment and indulgences; it is a plane meant for action and for your enlightenment. That is the purpose of life in the earth plane. For the purpose of enjoyments and pleasures, the Lord has created another plane, called *swarga*, the heavens. That is another plane altogether, while this earth plane is a *karma bhumi*, or a plane of action. As this is a plane of action, actions are to be done in this manner with a spirit of sacrifice.

Thus when action is well done with the spirit of sacrifice, then it is truly done. So it is with this spirit that we have to get into action. Therefore, every action is to be done as a sacrifice. You know very well what sacrifices you do in the world to keep your family going. But if you can understand this spirit in all actions that you do, then that is what is expected of you, as a *yagna*, as a sacrifice.

Thus the very action itself is dedicated to the Lord. In fact, this is the interpretation of the great Shankara himself. Shankara in his interpretation says that these actions are to be done with a sense of dedication unto Vishnu. Vishnu means God. All actions are to be dedicated and offered as an oblation unto God. Thus it is a *yagna*. "*Yagno vai vishn.*" *Yagna* is God. Normally, ignorant people perform ritualistic sacrifices and offer it to the gods. But here the whole of your life full of action, is to be offered and dedicated to the Divine. So with such dedication, if you were to perform your functions and duties then that is said to be a *yagna*.

Then Krishna further says, "What results out of this? If you are so able to live in this manner, and go about performing your actions in this manner, as a *yagna*, as a sacrifice, then what is the outcome of it?" He says in the next verse:

****

सहयज्ञाः प्रजाः सृष्ट्वा पुरोवाच प्रजापतिः ।
अनेन प्रसविष्यध्वमेष वोऽस्त्विष्टकामधुक् ॥ १० ॥

Sahayagnaaha prajaaha srestva purovaaca prajaapatihi |
Anena prasavisyadtwamesha voastuistakaamadhuk ||

Having created beings along with sacrifices, the Creator said long ago, may you increase (prosper) by this, may it give you the desired desirables. (10)

****

The Lord of all beings is the Creator. What did he do? He created beings along with sacrifices. Sacrifices here means your daily obligative duties. Because every *karma* is to be done as a *yagna*, "sacrifice." Every action is to be performed as a sacrifice. Therefore, the Creator created you along with your functions and duties which are to be gone through as a sacrifice. You are to live your life with the spirit of sacrifice and go through actions with the spirit of sacrifice. Prajapatihi, the Lord of all beings, created all beings, along with these obligative actions and functions, and said may you enrich yourself by the performance of actions with a spirit of sacrifice.

By so performing your actions as a sacrifice, what will transpire and what will you benefit by that? You will become more and more prosperous, by the spirit of sacrifice in the living of life. The law of life is, the more you give, the more you get back. People don't know this secret. It's a law of life. The more you give in sacrifice, out of the very virtue of that sacrifice, the more comes to you. That's a universal law.

Therefore, by performing actions in this manner as a sacrifice, the net result is, it helps you to increase, and become more prosperous, and obtain all what you have to obtain. Indeed it opens the door from all quarters of the world for your well being. Out of that merit acquired, all things come unto you. It is in this manner that you are to live life and attain your prosperity and well-being.

This method of going through life and life's activities and functions as a sacrifice, is a great *yagna*, which gives you all the desirable things. All the desires that you have or the desirable things that you have wanted, come to you by and by in course of time. Such a way of living life is a great sacrifice – *yagna,* which is the giver of all that is desirable, like the mythological cow which is a giver of everything that you wish.

In the Indian mythological tradition, there was such a cow, and it is said to have the face of a woman, the body of a cow, and the wings of a bird. And this cow was apparently in the possession of the sage Vashista, and is said to have given everything he wanted. This life which you are going through, along with the various actions, is allegorically comparable to such a cow, which is capable of giving all the desirable things in life.

You may have desired and wanted many things in the subconscious of your mind. Thus as you keep on living your life and performing all your functions as a sacrifice in the manner mentioned, then that very action which is being performed by you as a *yagna* is comparable to this mythical cow, which gives you all the desirable things that you need in life. The more you give and share with the world, the more the world shares with you. Thus there is bounty and plenty in your life. And whatever you do, and whatever sacrifices you make in life, do not imagine that it is unknown. It is known by all the gods whose bounty would be upon you. Thus whatever sacrifices and good things that you have done in the world, is all known, by the gods and the presiding cosmic forces. They know and understand. And then it comes back to you in ten-fold or hundred-fold. Therefore, this sacrifice is to be treated as that which is going to give you all the desired things in life.

And then further he says, in the eleventh verse:

****

देवान् भावयतानेन ते देवा भावयन्तु वः ।
परस्परं भावयन्तः श्रेयः परमवाप्स्यथ ॥ ११ ॥

Devanbhavayataanena te devaa bhavayantu vaha |
Parasparam bhavayantaha sreyaha paramavaapsyatha ||

By this the *devas* (gods) are propitiated; the *devas* in turn
propitiate you.
Thus by mutually propitiating, thou shall attain the highest good.

(11)

****

By this sacrifice, which you are constantly performing, *devas*,
the gods, are pleased. You know very well that if your own children
were to go about their life with exemplary behavior and doing what
they have to do, then as their parent, you naturally get pleased by
your child's performance, and give him whatever he needs. It's a
natural law. You are pleased by the excellence in behavior and
performance of your own children.

In exactly the same manner, when you go about your life with
such dedication, then the *devas*, who are overlooking the entire
sphere of life, get pleased. Then those *devas* in turn, will now please
you, by giving you whatever you need. You in turn have pleased
them, by your spirit of duty. And therefore, they in turn, please you.
Thus, there is a mutual aspect of pleasing each other. You please the
devatas, gods, with your own excellence in behavior and in action
done as a sacrifice all the time, as you are doing what you are
supposed to do.

Don't imagine that you can bribe the *devatas*, the gods.
That's another interesting thing, which is very often ignorantly done
all over the world. All over the world you have the priests enticing

and tempting the people to do ritualistic sacrifices to please the gods, by making various offerings. As if these gods require such offerings. This is the genesis of priest-craft the world over. The priests tell you, "Give this offering to the gods, and the gods will be pleased." They tell you, "The gods like this and the gods like that. Lord Shiva likes this, and Lord Vishnu likes that." But Shiva has no likes and dislikes, but the priests tell you Shiva likes this, and therefore you give offerings to Lord Shiva. Then the minute you bribe these *devatas*, or gods, do you think the *devatas* get pleased by that? Certainly not. This is clear bribery indeed. Therefore that's no way to please the gods. But the *devatas* are pleased by the way you have lived your life, and done your duties.

Suppose your son is naughty, and the little chap wants something out of you. He comes and gives you certain things and a few other articles which he has. In the first place, you don't need his money, and his articles, and you'll be wondering what is he up to now? Or if your son were to stand in front of you and were to recite, "Oh my great father, thou art glorious indeed, incomparable, and thou oh mother, you are so gracious and wonderful indeed." Now you'll be wondering what is he up to? So the *devatas* are not subject to this sort of praise or bribery. They are pleased by your way of life, the way you are performing your actions, and the way your thought patterns and emotions are functioning.

Thus, mutually taking care of each other, you attain to your ultimate well-being. In course of time, thou shall attain the supreme state.

In fact, when we use the word *devatas* here, we must understand that there is a *devata* which is a paramount *devata* - the supreme God. So whatever you offer, only goes to him directly. The receiver of all offerings is the paramount *devata*, the supreme God-head itself. The Great Spirit, as the American Indians would like to phrase.

By virtue of the excellence of your life and all what you have done, the grace of God comes to you. All good, all capacities and power flow only from God. The Source of all and of everything. Even the *devatas*, gods, know that in whatever functions they perform, they derive the capacity to do so only from the supreme God-head itself.

But as far as the *devatas* are concerned, it is said that the presiding deity of the eyes is said to be the Surya *devata*. Of the hands the deity is said to be Indra *devata*, and Vishnu is said to be the *devata* of the legs. Agni is said to be the *devata* for speech.

Thus, if you were to keep on abusing everyone, naturally what happens? That *devata*, who is now overlooking that sphere, gets displeased, and the power of speech in you goes away. It is withdrawn. If a person were to go about kicking people, then the deity withdraws the ability of that person to function with that limb. Hence these *devatas* oversee the corresponding functions in the scheme of things. And they all derive their power and capacity to so function from the supreme God-head itself.

That is why, in one of the Upanishads, it is mentioned, that a celestial being appeared in front of all the *devatas*. They were awe struck by that, and wanted to know who it was. When they approached it, the supreme God-head who had appeared in that celestial form, asked the *devatas*, "What power, what capacity have you?"

So the wind-god, Vaya *devata* said, "I can lift and carry away everything."

The fire-god, Agni devata said, "I can burn everything and reduce it to ashes."

Then the supreme God-head who had appeared in the form of the celestial being said, "If that is so, go ahead and do it. Let me see." They were not able to do so.

Thus it produced a piece of grass in front of those *devatas* and said, "Oh, wind-god, Vaya *devata*, if you think you are mighty and can take away everything, try to lift this blade of grass." It was unable to do so.

The Agni *devata* said, "I could burn everything."

"If that be the case, burn this grass."

It was unable to do so, as they all derive their power to so function from God, and when God withdraws that capacity, one becomes powerless. Every creature in the world derives its power to function only from the supreme God-head. Not only the *devatas* - even you too, derive your power, from the God-head. Hence understand this, and never function in the world with pride and arrogance.

Therefore, we are all obligated to the Divine. Thus, every action that you do as a sacrifice goes to that supreme deity the God-head. And it is out of the blessings of that, that all blessings come to you, because it is the Source.

Therefore, we should always be thankful to the Divine, for whatever blessings we have in life, however small the blessings be. It is only when we appreciate the little blessings, that the big blessings follow. I have rarely heard people say, that they have not been blessed by the Lord in some form or the other. Nearly everyone says, "Yes, the Lord has been kind to me at some time or the other in my life." Even a man who is in difficulty says that too.

But if you can have that blessed feeling all through your life, your life would be a blessing and you will be able to live in the world with humility, and without arrogance and pride as a beautiful soul. You could go about functioning in the world, knowing well that all the blessings and good things that you have in the world, come from the Divine. The Divine in turn will bless you evermore for your noble attitude. Everything comes to you, not because you deserve it, or do not deserve it, but comes to you for whatever purpose beyond human comprehension.

So with good grace, accept whatever comes into your life. And live your life in that manner. Live your life as a sacrifice, going through your functions and duties as a sacrifice. So if you can live with this idea that life itself is a sacrifice and that all actions are to be done as a sacrifice, then you'll have a different perspective towards life itself.

Life is to be lived with seriousness, because there is a purpose and a meaning to life. So with all dignity you have to live life, and go about life's purpose, for whatever you are meant to live for. By that life becomes meaningful, and can be lived with purpose and dignity. And the purpose is to do, whatever you are meant to do. Thus, in this manner, the idea of *yagna*, or sacrifice has been put across in the scriptures.

Verses 12 - 16

Lord Krishna had introduced a new concept as to what is signified and understood by the term *yagna*, sacrifice. The living of life and life's activities are to be treated as a *yagna*, a sacrifice. All life's functions ought to be gone through with a spirit of sacrifice. When a person performs his actions well with dedication, then that action is a sacrifice. Notwithstanding the results which may accrue out of it, he does those actions and functions because he has to do it, and therefore he is going to do it.

In such a spirit, all life's activities are to be gone through. Then the living of life itself, by virtue of that, becomes a sacrifice. In a narrow ritualistic sense, the term *yagna* means a ritual performed by pagan priests, in a sacrificial altar. But herein Krishna is trying to bring out a wider and a universal meaning to the word *yagna*, wherein every one of life's activities, can be converted into a *yagna*, a sacrifice. By performing any action as a sacrifice, it naturally becomes a *yagna*. By this, what happens? He says in the next verse:

****

इष्टान् भोगान्हि वो देवा दास्यन्ते यज्ञभाविताः ।
तैर्दत्तानप्रदायैभ्यो यो भुङ्क्ते स्तेन एव सः ॥ १२ ॥

Istaanbhogaan hi vo devaa daasyante yagna bhaavitaah |
Tair dattaan apradaayibhyo yo bhungte stena eva sah ||

Those *devas* (gods) being pleased with sacrifices will give the desired enjoyments.
Who enjoys the delectables given by them without giving in return is verily a thief. (12)

****

By virtue of these sacrifices, the *devas*, gods, in turn are pleased. You have done what you ought to have done and have lived life, in the way life is expected to be lived. As a result the gods, the *devas*, are pleased. Then they offer you the delectables of life.

A normal person in the world has many desirable things which he may subconsciously wish for. If you ask a man what he would like to have, it will take him time to consider what he wants, because he has so many things that he wants that he cannot give you an instant reply. He is overwhelmed by his desires, so he is momentarily incapable of giving an instant reply. But on the other hand, if you ask a person who has no desires, as to what he wants, he too will be scratching his head to think what he wants, as there is nothing in particular he wants. What an irony life is. One person is unable to reply because he has nothing particular to want, and the other person is also unable to reply because he has so many wants.

So all those little wants that you have been wishing subconsciously and wanting in your life, the *devatas* will bestow upon you. Your little boy may express to you what he wants, because you don't have the capacity to know what is in his mind. But the *devatas* know very well what things you want, and the desirable things you chase in life. After all, you are a human being living in the world, and hence have your aspirations in life. Therefore you are entitled to the goods of the world. It is not that you are supposed to live like a hermit. No, not at all. It is not possible. Therefore, you are naturally entitled to the good things of life. That's perfectly natural. *Dharma, arta, kama,* and *moksha* are the four aspirations of life. You are entitled to these four. To acquire *Dharma,* so that one can be virtuous; to acquire *arta,* the goods of life, so that one can live comfortably; to fulfill one's desires, so that one can be happy, and to long for *moksha,* so that one can get liberated from this universe and

73

attain enlightenment.

By *dharma*, you are to lead a *dharmic* life. By *artha*, you are entitled to acquire and cherish the desirable things of life. That is why Lord Krishna told Arjuna, 'When you take part in this righteous war, which is your duty at this particular moment, in case you die, you will obtain the warrior's heaven. But in case you defeat the enemy, you will enjoy this kingdom.' By that he is not telling him not to enjoy and partake of the good things in life.

Therefore, those *devas* will be pleased by your good life and your good deeds, and your life of sacrifice. Thereafter, all the desirable things come to you in due course in life. That being the case, naturally go through the operations and the living of your life. Thus in whatever form anything is given to us we must have the good grace to accept, and be thankful for it. Therefore, whatever blessings and good things that have come to us, we should be thankful for that. Thus having received the good things of life, we must also have the good sense to give back. Therefore a part of what we receive, should also be given and distributed to one and all. In your thanks, you share whatever you have. You share your wealth around you. So when you keep on acquiring wealth, you must also have the good sense, wisdom, and the graciousness to share what you have with others too. Generally you are prepared to share what you have with your immediate family, but that alone will not do. What about the human family? What about all the beings and creatures around you? You must learn to share with all around you. So when you are so able to share, by virtue of that, the gods and the *devas* are pleased. By that, good will befall you.

There is a nice story with respect to this. There was a businessman, and as all businessmen are, they make interesting promises that if they do well in their business, they will give part of it to God. And very often a student also makes such a promise that if he passes the exam, he will break a coconut at the temple. Fortunately, the coconut is broken only outside the temple, and not on the deity. It is a way of giving thanks, an expression of gratitude. It so happened that the businessman did well in business. He had now to fulfill his promise, which was a thousand *rupees* which would be given to the deity in the temple at Badrinath.

It so happened that there was a *sadhu*, a *swami*, who was going that way. So he asked him, to take the thousand *rupees* and give it to the temple. In the good old days, a thousand *rupees* was a lot of money. Now this was an interesting *swami*. As he was passing through, wherever he found poor people in need he began distributing the thousand *rupees*. Thus he distributed the money to the poor on the way. By the time he reached the temple at Badrinath, he was left with one *rupee*. So he put that money in the donation box of the temple.

In the meantime, the businessman had heard that the *swami*, instead of putting the money into the temple box, had been giving it to the poor on the way. Therefore, he went after the *swami* because he had to fulfill his promise. When he reached Rishikesh, which was on the way, he had a dream. In that dream, God himself appeared and told him, "I have received 999 *rupees*, but there is still a balance of one *rupee* left." The 999 *rupees* to the poor was received. But the one *rupee* in the temple box goes to the temple authorities. Therefore, whatever and whenever a person gets in life, in the form of wealth, he must have the good sense to also distribute a part of it to the poor and the needy around him. That benevolent action is called a sacrifice. So those good things which have been given to you by the blessings of the good Lord, must also be given out and distributed and not hoarded. By that, the good Lord Himself is pleased with you by your nobility.

Thus, a person who does not do this, is *stena eva sa*, is

verily a thief. Whatever "blessings" a person has in any form, if he were to use it for himself, selfishly and exclusively for his own personal purpose, then Krishna says, 'Such a person is verily a thief.' A thief - because he is supposed to share with all around as he is not getting only for himself, as he is also a member of the human community.

Whenever you get something, you are told by your elders, "Kindly share it with others." Even as a child when a close relative gives you a present, he tells you to, "Share it with the others in the family." In adult life you are not told that, but you must have the good sense to understand that, and share with all around. Understand that when the Lord gives you the things in life, it is to be implicitly understood that part of it is to be shared.

Because you are living in a collective world, and in a collective society. You are not an independent being. For your own existence, there is collective set-up. Therefore, you must have the good sense to contribute to the world around you, because you are receiving many things from the world around you. For your own comfort, and for your own well-being, many things are coming to you, which is the contribution of the collective society. Therefore, if you do not give back to the society, you become a thief. As you are getting from the society, therefore, you should also give something back to the society.

When everyone gives back to the world, the world in turn is capable of giving you ever more and more. That is a law of life. And a person who does not do it, and lives his own selfish life, receiving and pocketing everything, is said to be verily a thief. That is why in all cultures of the world, charity is part of noble living. But this concept taught by Lord Krishna is more than charity. It is an integral part of man's duty and way of living life. Furthermore, when things are to be given, they are to be given with love and consideration for the well-being and happiness of the people who receive. You also should be happy in giving, and see to it that the people around you are also made happy. When everyone is happy, there is happiness all around the world. This is how one should live.

In the living of life, the joy of giving is far more wonderful than the joy of receiving. It is a remarkable thing which opens one to God and happiness.

There is a great joy in giving and making people happy. You know this well in a family set-up, wherein you want to give to your own immediate loved ones whom you love. You are happy to give because you love them and therefore, want to give. You want to see happiness around you. In the same way too, there should be this cosmic, universal love. That loving feeling must come into you, and your heart must expand, and have the capacity to embrace the world around you. Then you will have the natural tendency to give around you. You will be happy to give, whenever the need arises. Then only will you expand and grow into Divinity. The other is contraction. When you want to receive and grab everything, it is contraction. But when you give, you expand into the infinite, and become the infinite, Divine itself. It is the way to grow and become the infinite. Therefore, such a way of life is most desirable.

Then he says:

****

यज्ञशिष्टाशिनस्सन्तो मुच्यन्ते सर्वकिल्बिषैः ।
भुञ्जते ते त्वघं पापा ये पचन्त्यात्मकारणात् ॥ १३ ॥

Yagnasistaasinaha santo muchyante sarvakilbishihi |
Bhunjete te twagam paapaa ye pachantyaatmakaaranaath ||

The good people who partake the remnants (balance) of the "sacrifice" are released from all sins.

Those who selfishly intake (live), verily eat sin.   (13)

****

That person who is so able to live his life performing all his life functions and activities as a sacrifice, and is living his life as such, is a meritorious soul. He is said to be a *sadhu*, a good being. He is a *sadhu*, because he has the character of a *sadhu*. A person who is a benefactor to the world around him is said to be a *sadhu*. That is why holy-beings are referred to by the word *sadhus*, because they are naturally good beings, full of love, compassion and kindness.

A person who partakes of his food, having first offered to others is doing a *yagna*. As he first offers to the living gods as a sacrifice, and then partakes of whatever is left. Such a person is said to be taking the remnants of the sacrifice. As he has first offered things to others, it is a sacrifice, and after the sacrifice is over, partakes of whatever is left and takes it as sanctified food. It is in such a manner that one should partake and consume the good things of life as well. After having offered it as an oblation, and then after the others have partaken, he also partakes of it.

In the Indian tradition, first of all the guest is fed as he is a manifest god, and thereafter you take your food. For, whatever food that has been prepared of course is prepared for your taking too. But first you feed the guest, and see that he has been fed and thereafter, you partake of what is left. That is the remnants of the food, which has been taken by you after having made it as a sacrifice unto someone. That becomes a sacrifice, a *yagna*. Those people, whose entire life is lived in such a manner of sacrifice wherein all their actions have become a sacrifice - are doing a constant *yagna*. Thereafter whatever they get in life has come as a remnant of that sacrifice, as a follow-through. Whatever function that you do in each one of your activities, either in the kitchen, or in the office, or in the garden outside during the day, and whatever you get thereafter now becomes a remnant of the sacrifice which you are constantly performing in your life. Therefore, what happens to you by that?

By that, he says, "*Muchyante sarva kilbishihi.*" By virtue of living your life with such a spirit of sacrifice, you get released from all sins, wittingly or unwittingly, knowingly or unknowingly, committed. You get absolved of them. Because your whole life has been a sacrifice, and by virtue of that, you have acquired merit or *punya*, and this will neutralize any error, any commissions or omissions, which you may have gone through, knowingly or unwittingly. Thus it absolves you.

But on the other hand, those who do not go through their life's activities as a sacrifice, but live a selfish, self-centered life, ingest sin. Whatever they partake in life is vitiated and tainted by sin. Thus Krishna says, "*Bhunjante agam papa pachanti atmakaaranaath.*" 'Sinful digest sin who live for themselves.' That means, all things of life have to be shared by one and all, in a just manner. If not, it becomes a sinful life. Thus it is clear that a selfish life becomes a life of sin. Those who digest and take everything for their own personal pleasures and enjoyments, live a life of sin. For such people everything is a one-way traffic wherein they are prepared to receive, but never to give.

It is a law of life that each one is a member of a cosmic set-up. You cannot live by yourself in this world. You are a part of a community, the human community which is the human family to which you belong. Since you are part and parcel of the cosmic family, therefore it is part of your duty to give back to the community from whom you receive, as a constant interaction is always taking place. As you receive, so should you also give. As you keep on receiving, to that proportion should you keep on giving, too. This is the law of life, and that person who does not go through this law of life, is said to be a sinner, absorbing sins within himself. It is certainly a most

79

undesirable way of living.

Therefore, you must live by the good knowledge which has been revealed to you in the scriptures as to how to live life. Because you have not come into this world only to go through life as if it were a pleasure-ground. You have come here to learn your lessons in this world, and go through life as an experience, for growth and for further spiritual development. This is a *karma bhumi*, and not a *bhoga bhumi*. That is, this is a plane of action, and not a plane of enjoyment. But man has an ingenious mind, to try to convert it into a plane of enjoyment, and he pays for it! It is always seen that when man gets into a life of indulgence and enjoyments, decadence sets in. The fall of the Roman Empire is a classic example of this. A life of indulgence and decadence makes a person emotionally, mentally, and psychologically sick. He becomes a sick being, sick in mind. But a life of hard work strengthens and fortifies the mind and soul.

Therefore, man must learn to temper his instincts, temper his life, and live by the good words and good knowledge of the scriptures, which have instructed him how to live life. That is called education. You have come into this world to be educated, educated about life and the living of life in a noble manner. And it is this education, that we are seeking here.

There is an interesting concept in the next two verses, how prosperity comes to a nation. There is a law of life, and people belonging to a nation, should follow this law, so that the entire nation can become prosperous, and their well-being gets taken care. That procedure is being mentioned in the next two verses. So he says:

****

अन्नाद्भवन्ति भूतानि पर्जन्यादन्नसंभवः ।
यज्ञाद्भवति पर्जन्यो यज्ञः कर्मसमुद्भवः ॥ १४ ॥

Annaatbhavanti bhutaani parjenyadanna sambhavaha |
Yagnaadbhavathi parjenyo yagnaha karmasamudbhavaha ||

Beings originate from food; from rains come food; from sacrifices
 transpire rains.
Sacrifice arises from action. (14)
****

कर्म ब्रह्मोद्भवं विद्धि ब्रह्माऽक्षरसमुद्भवम् ।
तस्मात्सर्वगतं ब्रह्म नित्यं यज्ञे प्रतिष्ठितम् ॥ १५ ॥

Karma brahmodbhavam viddhi brahmaaksharasamudbhavam |
Tasmatsarvagatam brahma nityam yagne prathistitam ||

Action originates from *brahma*; *brahma* arises from the imperishable
(absolute).
Therefore the all-pervasive *brahma* is established in sacrifice.

(15)

****

This is a universal law of life, meant for the prosperity of the
nation, and whole of mankind.

He says, *"Annaat Bhavanti Bhutani."* Of course, it is well
known out of food, come all beings; all creatures take birth and come
into existence. Having taken birth, they are further nourished by
food. For the food that you eat is converted into flesh and blood,
and then from that to marrow. Thereafter, the essence of the marrow
gets converted or transformed as semen. Thus the food has been
transformed into semen. Then the semen, is ejected into the woman
and soon after becomes the newborn baby. So it is out of food that
the creatures are born. The physical body itself is the product of
food, and is sustained by food.

But for the food to grow, rains are needed. Only when there

are rains, is there water. So when there are rains, naturally the plants grow, and therefore food crops come. So the cause of the food that you are eating is rains. If there were no rains in the world, there would be no food. Therefore, *parjanyaat anna sambhavaha.* So from the rains, the food comes.

But as far as the rains are concerned, everybody knows the natural laws by which rains come. When the sun evaporates the waters of the ocean, then those waters become clouds; then those clouds in turn fall as rain. This everybody knows. But then there are periods in life, in spite of the fact that the oceans are all there, it does not rain. And sometimes there is excess rain. There is more rain than you want, and there are destructive floods everywhere. And when there are no rains, that too is not very desirable. But this phenomenon happens at all times, all over the world.

But then, there are certain unseen laws totally distinct and separate from the physical laws by which rain comes. There are also certain unseen laws which bring forth rain. For whatever that transpires in the world, there are unseen laws also operating. That is why in the world, in spite of the best efforts that couples make in their life to bring forth children, they are unable to do so. If not, they should have a child every year, but that does not happen so. Some people are also childless in spite of all their efforts. This is so as there are certain other unseen laws, unknown to man, which are contributive factors in the begetting of a child. So too in a similar manner for the rains to come, many unseen factors are operative in the universe. So it is said, "*Yagnaath bhavati parjanya.*" Through sacrifice, the rains come.

There are two forms of sacrifice. We will go through the first form. The first form of sacrifice is what we have discussed as *yagna.* When a particular nation of people go about leading a life of sacrifice, wherein their living of life has been a sacrifice, then they have led their lives in a meritorious manner, and such a life is called a *yagna* or a life of sacrifice. As for example when a woman sacrifices her time, energy, and resources for the well-being of her family, then she is doing a sacrifice for the maintenance of the human race. A mother is always self-sacrificing. By virtue of that, her life is a life of sacrifice. This is the concept of *yagna* - sacrifice, as presented in the Bhagavad Gita by Lord Krishna. That is the way man or woman should live his or her life. Always keeping in view the well-being of all concerned. Life thus lived promotes harmony, well-being, and happiness in the world for oneself and for all.

By virtue of that sacrifice as a *yagna*, merit - *punya*, is generated. Another term for *punya* is *apurva*. That is the unseen potential of accumulated merit which awaits fructification. Thus whatever good that one does, eventually generates merit in the person. So also the collective *punya* or merit of all people put together, is said to be a collective merit, and it is this merit which now helps to bring about the rains. It is that subtle, unknown factor, which promotes all the good things in life for one and all, that induces the cause for the initial formation of rain, by bringing about the rain forming clouds.

But in the world this beautiful concept of sacrifice has been misunderstood, and the net result being that the pagan priests the world over have induced and made the people participate in pagan rituals and pagan worship of gods, in various forms of sacrifices involving either animate or inanimate substances.

Then the other idea is, actually there is a sacrifice which is meant to bring about rain. Soon after that, the rains come. It is not often done today.

In fact, there was a very well-known *swami*, about forty years ago in Rishikesh, who performed this ritual to bring about rain.

And it was said that soon after that, the rains did come, where there were no clouds earlier. So even the disbelievers are made to believe, when the actual thing takes place. It is a procedure. So in the same way also in a general sense, the collective *punya* or merit of all the people living there, induce rain.

That is how, in the Mahabharata episode in Indian history, the Pandavas who were sent to exile for thirteen years in the forest, and one year more to live in incognito, were discovered. During the incognito period if they were detected, then they were to once again redo the thirteen years. Thus Duryodhana was very keen on finding out where the Pandavas were living incognito. In life it is found that even a wicked man gets clever advice, so someone told him that Yudhishthira of the Pandavas would be found where there would be abundance. Wherever Yudhishthira goes, there would be abundance.

So Duryodhana was searching for that particular city, which was full of abundance, because that must be the probable place where Yudhishthira would be. As he being a very meritorious and exalted soul, wherever he went, there would be prosperity and well-being, as his entire life was a *yagna*. Every single act that he was doing was a *yagna*, a sacrifice. By virtue of that he had generated great merit.

That is why it is said, "India is a blessed land." That is because, now and then in the four corners of the blessed land, great souls have walked about. They are the holy beings, the men of God, the great saints of India. They had walked about, and had sanctified the earth of India. They had blessed the land of India by their mere presence, and existence. Therefore it is called the blessed land. Not because of the people living there, but in spite of them who comprise the greater mass of India. It is said if you have one great soul in a country or region, that one person is enough to sanctify that area. Here too, it was the same case with Yudhishthira. That is why he was called Dharmaputra, the son of Dharma, the very embodiment of *dharma* itself. Therefore, wherever he was, there itself is *dharma*, and there would be prosperity and rain aplenty. So it is in that manner that Duryodhana discovered the probable city in which they dwelt incognito.

So *yagna karma samudbhava. Yagna*, sacrifice, only becomes a sacrifice, when actions are done. When any action is performed with the spirit of sacrifice, then that action becomes a *yagna*. Thus one does not have to perform a separate *yagna*, but on the contrary, any action that is done spontaneously becomes a *yagna*, when done with the spirit of sacrifice. So it is in this manner that *yagna* is to be performed by an individual.

This truth is very well illustrated, in a beautiful incident in the Hindu epic Mahabharata. After the Mahabarata war was over, Yudhishthira performed a religious ritual, traditionally called a *yagna* in India.

At its conclusion, along came a mongoose. But it was a very unusual mongoose, with one part of its body golden, and the other part its natural color. That mongoose came to the *yagna* hall and overheard people say that, "There has not been a greater *yagna* than this."

On hearing it, the mongoose said, "All of you are liars indeed."

The people were wonderstruck. They said, "How do you say that!"

Then the mongoose said, "I came here to this *yagna* and rolled on the ground here, where the religious ceremony had been performed. But, alas I find that the other part of my body has not turned golden." One half turned golden, when it came in contact with another great *yagna* - sacrifice - performed elsewhere.

The the mongoose said, "I was in an area, where there was famine. There lived a poor man, with his wife and two little children. They had only a small loaf of bread left for survival. They cut it into four small slices, and were about to consume it. At that moment came a hungry man clamoring for food. He was in a fervor of hunger. The man gave him one slice of the bread. When the man wanted more, he was given the second slice; having consumed it, the heat of hunger and of starvation was so intense, that he wanted even more. So the family willingly parted with the remaining two slices as well. They had no more food left, and in a few days they too died of starvation in the famine-ridden area. This gracious and great act was a sacrifice. Thus a great *yagna* - sacrifice - had been performed."

The mongoose continued. "I happened to come that way, and accidentally a part of my body touched or came in contact with minute traces of the crumbs of bread fallen on the floor. To my utter surprise, that part turned golden, as it touched the remnants of the great sacrifice. Since then, I have been searching for another great *yagna*, to turn the balance of my body golden, but to no avail thus far."

So sacrifice depends on the circumstances of the individual sacrificing, that is the capacity of your sacrifice. For a billionaire to give a thousand dollars is nothing. That is a sacrifice, if a person had only a thousand dollars, and if he were to give away a half of it. Therefore here also it was a great sacrifice, wherein the whole family perished after giving up their last supper. So the mongoose said, "I happened to come that way, and I happened to roll over on the ground on which these people had performed their sacrifice, and it so happened that wherever my body rolled, and came in contact with traces of food, became golden. Thereafter, I thought to myself, 'Let me see if there will be another great sacrifice, *yagna*, which will equal this.' I heard about the great *yagna* being performed by Yudhishthira here with pomp and pagentry, but I am sorry to tell you the other part of my body has not turned golden."

Thus the concept of sacrifice is what has to be understood and appreciated. You are given an opportunity in life to perform *yagna* every moment of your life. And it is this *yagna* which goes to sanctify and ennoble your life. Life-situations are placed in life, wherein you should go through life activities as a *yagna* - sacrifice, in due proportion to your own individual capacity.

Thus he says, *yagna karma samudbhavam.* So *yagna* transpires or takes place out of the performance of action, done with the spirit of sacrifice. In order to perform these actions, where do you get your authority? Of course everybody does actions in the world, right and wrong actions, proper and improper actions, virtuous and non-virtuous actions. But in order to know what you are supposed to do and what you are not supposed to do, where do you derive your authority and sanction from? There must be guide-lines to live life. Because if you were to live by your instincts, impulses, and urges, you are bound to err in actions. So there must be guide-lines to regulate your urges and instincts, and live life by certain norms, and principles. Where do you derive these guide-lines and laws of life, by which you will be able to live and go through your function of life? Lord Krishna says, "That is derived and obtained from the scriptures. *Karma brahma samudbhavam.*" That is, actions originate from Brahma. Brahma means the Vedas, the scriptures. The Vedas deal with the do's and don'ts of life. Thus the authority for actions is obtained from the Vedas, which reveal to you what should be done, and what should not be done.

The word *Brahma* stands here for the Vedas. Vedas means the scriptures. Vedas represent action and is said to be the *karma khanda* section, which primarily deals with the performance of ritualistic action. Like the Ten Commandments of the Christians, they also enjoin the do's and don'ts of life.

Then where does the scripture come from? It comes from God, *brahma akshara samudbhavam*. God reveals the Truths of life. He reveals the Truth about Himself and of the world. The word *akshara* stands for the Divine. It means, that which does not perish, which is eternal, and everlasting. There is only one thing which is eternal and everlasting. That is the Divine. So it is from God that the scriptures manifest. The scriptures in turn too, reveal God. God manifests the scriptures to reveal Himself.

Don't imagine that the scriptures of the world are man-made, or are the product of the human mind. The substance of it is God-given. It is revealed by God unto mankind. That is why it is called a revelation. It reveals to you truths, about life, and the ultimate reality. It contains a unique message. The message that God is. God says, 'I AM. I EXIST IN YOU TOO. KNOW IT AND BE BLESSED IN KNOWING WHO YOU REALLY ARE. THOU ART A SPARK OF ME, WHOLE AS I AM.' If not for this message, man would not know that God is, and what his source is. Thus knowing this, man's life falls in place. It is a comfort to know who one is, and where one belongs.

Who is that who can reveal to you truths of the ultimate reality? Who else but God. God who has created the universe, has also revealed the nature of the universe, and the nature of Himself. His revelation is an effortless process. It is an effortless knowledge intrinsically present within Him, manifesting itself at all times, like the effortless breath of man. Just as your breathing is an effortless process, so natural to you and to your nature, so too, God's knowledge and its revelation is effortlessly inherent to His Being. Thus the revealed word transpires from God.

Therefore, the scriptures are said to be infallible in its teachings and guidance to mankind. It reveals to you all about the mystery of life. The scriptures also shed light on many aspects of life and living. As such the knowledge of the scriptures is based on its performance in everyday life. That is why Krishna says, "*Sarvagatam brahma yagne pratistitam.*" That is, the all-pervasive, meaning the all-revealing scripture is based on its performance. Of course, if man were not to live by the words of the scripture, then it would be mute, and as good as in the closet. Because the scriptures would be mute until they get translated as a dynamic expression of life. If somebody comes and tells you, "Of course, we too have the scriptures, it is in our cupboards." Of what use is it? The scripture becomes dynamic when you are living the scripture. It becomes a dynamic expression of your life, only if you were to live by the words of the scripture. Hence the scripture is established in its performance, and thus paves the way to Enlightenment. If not, it is dead.

And part of the words of the scripture is to get into action. Action performed as a *yagna*. That is, action to be done with the spirit of sacrifice. Therefore, the scriptures are established in the *yagna* or the sacrifice that you perform every moment of your life. Because then you are living it.

Then what happens to the person who does not follow this divine cosmic law which has been set in motion?

****

एवं प्रवर्तितं यज्ञं नानुवर्तयतीह यः ।
अघायुरिन्द्रियारामो मोघं पार्थ स जीवति ॥ १६ ॥

Evam pravartitam chakram naanuvartayateeha yaha |
Aghaayurindriyaaraamo mokham paartha sa jeevati ||

That person who does not observe here the thus established sequential laws of life leads a sinful life, is sensuous, and lives his life in vain. (16)

****

Thus the cosmic wheel, the law of life, has been set in motion by the creator. And what is this law of life? Out of food are the beings born; and food comes from rain. The rains come out of *yagna*, that is performance of *karma* done with the spirit of sacrifice. And the *yagna* in turn is derived from the knowledge of the scriptures. The scriptures in turn are revealed or manifest from God. And the scriptures which show the way to God are based on action done with the spirit of sacrifice. Thus action translated as *yagna* leads to God. And *yagna* is the performance of action with the spirit of sacrifice. Therefore, he who does not follow this law which has been set for the welfare of man by the creator, is a sinner. His life is said to be a sinful life.

It is sinful for two reasons. One is, if he does not follow this law which has been set in motion in the universe, he violates the law laid down by the creator. Hence to have knowledge of it, he must take recourse to the scripture. If perchance he is not prepared to follow this law of life, he violates the law. Neither ignorance of it, nor the non-compliance of it, is an excuse in the eyes of the law. Thus he is a sinner. The word "sin" means, deviation from what is right.

Also by not doing what you are supposed to do (that is the second form), you obtain another sin; *pratya vaya dosha*, by the non-performance of an action. So when you don't do something, you have to be punished for not doing what you are supposed to do. Not-doing is one mistake. Then by virtue of not doing you incur a subsequent defect. Therefore, it is a double error indeed. And he says, the person's life is a life of sin when such a person lives a selfish, sensuous life for his own selfish purposes. He has not learned to live life, the way it ought to be lived. Therefore his life has been lived in vain.

90

Verses 17 - 20

It is the duty of people living in the world, to get into action and then perform those actions as a *yagna*. That means as a sacrifice. When actions are done with the spirit of sacrifice, then those actions sanctify one and become a *yoga* of action, *karma yoga*. For *karma yoga* one sacrifices, or renounces the fruits or results of one's endeavor. One performs actions as a matter of course, because they are meant to be done. One's focus is on the action awaiting to be done, and not on its outcome or result whatever it be. Thus one is action-oriented, and not result-conscious. This concept is what makes it a *yoga* of action. This concept of action is the principle spiritual discipline for people living an active life in the world.

But is it the case with one and all? No. It was previously mentioned that there are two types of individuals in the world, and with respect to each, their unique way of life is different. A person who is still a man of the world, a householder, possessed of many duties and functions and responsibilities, must live in the active society and go through his social functions and duties of life. On the other hand, for the individual who has obtained total *vairagya* or dispassion, his way of life is different. Such an individual, has no action whatsoever to do. All that he has to do is to withdraw from the active world, and get absorbed in the Divine, and be in a meditative state.

The person who is possessed of this natural *vairagya*, or dispassion from the world, has risen above mundane desires and ambitions which are the normal tendencies of the people of the world. Therefore he has nothing to achieve or perform in the world. Such a person naturally withdraws from active society, gets into a hermitage or into the jungles, and leads the life of a renunciate monk or hermit.

This individual has nothing else to do except to be self-absorbed in his Divine Nature. Dispassion is the primary requisite to be in such a contemplative state. Thus a renunciate is a hermit, or a monk who lives in a monastery or in the jungles. He is ever in a prayerful state, always in active contemplation. That is all that he does. He has no functions or social duties to go through. He has no further responsibilities. Others may think that he has, but he does not. They may presume that he may have responsibilities, but he does not. As his frame of mind has evolved into the higher perspectives of life, and is thereby governed by the spiritual laws of life.

Such a person is normally called "twice-born." "Twice-born" means he has undergone a psychological rebirth. The physical body which you have now is your first birth. But then later on, on account of the *punya*, or the meritorious life that you have led before, and on account of the various spiritual disciplines that you had gone through and also by the grace of God, the psychological birth, or rebirth transpires in an individual. At this point, his entire mental psyche undergoes a change. A psychological regeneration takes place. His mind-structure becomes refined and has become sensitive to the call of God. A yearning for God and Truth possesses his mind on account of the inner shift. His mind-stream yearns to go back to its God-Source. Such a person has been baptized by God. This is the true meaning of the concept, "He who has been baptized is saved."

In the Hindu tradition too, this is what is understood as the dawn of new *samskaras*; that is, new impressions and impulses. When by the grace of God an inner shift takes place with the regeneration of the mind, then the person becomes God-focused, and thus is said to be "twice-born." An inner psychological rebirth has taken place with the down of new *samskaras* or impressions. Such a person is only a true *Brahmana*. A person in whom the passions have cooled, and thereby is aspiring for God with all his heart and being. This is a far cry from the group of persons who are filled with worldly passions and desires and who profess themselves to be *Brahmins*, belonging to the so-called *Brahmin* caste in the Hindu structure of society. A mere outward ritualistic thread ceremony, *Upanayana*, does not confer or bring about a regeneration of one's impulses and nature, nor does it change the existing *samskaras* of a person.

For, there is a well-known and oft-quoted statement in the Vedas which state that, "*Janmana jaayate sudro samskarat dwijo bhavati.*" That is, all are born with unregenerate impulses (as *sudras*), but with the inflow of good impressions flooding the mind, become regenerated as a "twice-born." Thus with the regeneration of one's impulses, tendencies, and mind structure, one quests for God with one's whole heart, and not for the mundane things of the world. At this point a "twice-born" is naturally possessed of dispassion, *vairagya*. This is a sign by which a "twice-born" is to be recognized in the world. For the grace of God is upon him, and he responds to the call of God with all his heart and being.

It is at that time, this person renounces the active society. It is not that he renounces, he just walks away. Normal functionings just drop away from him.

So the state of renunciation is not a mental act, nor an intellectual decision, as to whether one should renounce or not. When a person has that doubt, then he should not renounce. As that doubt itself indicates that the dispassionate frame of mind has not yet come. When such a frame of mind transpires, then the person rises above normal worldly tendencies. Thus, dispassion is a state of mind and not an intellectual act. Renunciation is not a mental decision or an intellectual act. It is just like a little boy who was playing with marbles and toys, and when he grows a little older, does he say that, "I have renounced my marbles and toys?" He would be ashamed to even say that. In fact, they drop away, because he has outgrown them. In his mentality, he has obtained a certain amount of maturity by virtue of which he outgrows those tendencies.

Similarly also, in life too, it is the same phenomena. When a person matures psychologically, emotionally, and mentally; then he is a mature being and for such a person, by the grace of God, this particular state of dispassion transpires. Thus at this time, he outgrows the normal tendencies and functions of the world. Thereafter, this person has only one thing to do, and that is to be by himself, and be in a contemplative state. For which he gets away from active society. Thus, such a person only, is eligible to renounce active life in the worldly society.

Therefore, if somebody comes and asks you, "Should I renounce or not?" the answer is very clear, "No, you should not renounce." Because the moment that state comes, you don't have to ask anybody, for you just walk away. You don't need the sanction or permission of anybody.

Therefore, for such people, there are no actions whatsoever to do. If at all they have some action, it is only to be in a contemplative state and maintain their awareness in the reality, the truth of life. This is the meditative state. That is all that he has to do. Thereafter, through the practice of meditation, the person gets established in his Divine Nature. Lord Krishna is describing the nature of being of such a person in the next two verses. He says in the seventeenth verse:

****

यस्त्वात्मरतिरेव स्यादात्मतृप्तश्च मानवः ।
आत्मन्येव च सन्तुष्टस्तस्य कार्यं न विद्यते ॥ १७ ॥

94

Yestuvaatmaratireva syiyadaatmatriptasca maanavaha|
Aatmanyeva ca samtustastasya kaaryam na vidyate||

But the man who rejoices only in the Self, who is satisfied with the Self, who is happy in the Self alone, for him verily there is nothing to be done. (17)

****

A person naturally becomes self-absorbed, when he has no worldly inclinations and tendencies. Thus, naturally his mind would be only in the Divine; or rather in one's Divine Nature, which is one's true nature of being. One's true nature is the Self, referred to by the word *Atman* or *Brahman*. *Atman* is your true Self. Thus their awareness is in their true being, the Self. Therefore, such a person naturally revels in the *Atman, atma rati. Rati* means revels; he rejoices in the *Atman.*

Normally people's awareness is in the things of the world. They rejoice in the things of the world, and in the experiences of life and living. Where the heart is, there the mind is. So this is the tendency of a normal worldly man. But as far as this individual is concerned, since he is self-absorbed in the *Atman*, naturally that is where he rejoices. Hence *atma triptasca*, is satisfied in the self.

People obtain satisfaction when they come in contact with the things of the world, and have the experience thereof. Also in the same token, when people are deprived of the worldly things, they lose that satisfaction. But the spiritual seeker who is self-absorbed in the *Atman*, is satisfied in his own being.

He may be living in the forest, in a humble hut even with less than the barest necessities of life, totally content. People wonder how he is rejoicing himself and from where is his satisfaction coming from. There is nothing there, except the woods and the animals.

This man is deriving his pleasure and happiness by living such a way of life. When a person is self-absorbed in the *Atman*, a natural satisfaction and contentment comes from within. Thus he is content to be absorbed in the *Atman*, the Self.

Then he says, *"Atma santustasca."* His happiness is also in the *Atman*.

Normally people derive happiness when they have their own kith and kin around them. When their people are around them, along with all the worldly things, then that gives people contentment and happiness. Thus they are deriving their happiness from the external things outside. And if perchance they are deprived of that, they naturally lose their happiness. Because their happiness is dependent upon the presence or absence of the things around them.

So when something happens to any one of those situations, or pleasurable things in the form of either the wife has left him, or the husband has strayed away, or the house has gone, or the job has gone, or the children have gone astray, or they have had financial loss, immediately the sense of loss is felt and they lose their happiness. That itself will show you where their happiness is. So long as all these things are there, the happiness is there. When any one of them is missing, or something has gone wrong with any one of them, then and there itself they tend to lose their happiness. So it is quite clear that their happiness is based on the presence of all these things, within their proximity.

But as far as this individual is concerned, his *santusti*, happiness, is in the *Atman* itself. Because the *Atman*, the Self, is of the nature of happiness. Why is the wife dear to you? Why is the husband dear to you? Why are the children dear to you? The wife is dear, not for the sake of the wife. The husband is not dear for the sake of the husband. The children are dear not for the sake of the children. But because they bring about a frame of mind which induces joy, your joyous state of being, so dear to you. Since your own particular joyous state is so dear to you, therefore, these people are dear to you. They are dear not for their own sake, but for your sake.

That is why this truth is clearly mentioned in the "Brihadarenyaka Upanishad," in the form of a dialogue. Therein there is a discussion between the sage Yagnavalkya and his wife Maitreyi. The sage has already realized his own true Self, and feels that enough is enough of living in this world, and thereby wants to be totally immersed in his Divine Nature of being. For this he wants to isolate himself and remain totally self-absorbed in his Divine Nature.

Therefore, as he had two wives, he wanted to divide his assets between the two. Accordingly, he called his two wives and told them his intentions. To this, Maitreyi, who was one of the two, asked him a question, "Do you think that, by obtaining this I would be happy?"

He said, "No."

Then she said, "If that be the case, I do not want them. I want that which will make me happy." What is the source of happiness?

Then he gives this explanation, "The wife is not dear for the sake of the wife." So long as the wife is nice and fine, she is dear because your own self, the *atman* is dear to you. Therefore the wife is dear to you. The husband is dear so long as he is dear to your own self. The day your self feels that he is no more dear to you, then you know what to do. So here also it is the same thing. Everything you have, is dear not for the sake of that particular thing, but for the sake of your own self. Your own self is that which is most dear to you.

Now if the house is on fire, and if the family members are trapped inside with all your worldly goods; if there is time, you would try to rescue them. If not, you will leave them to their fate, as your life or rather, you, are more dear to yourself. If perchance your little child is caught in the fire, you will stand outside wailing, "Somebody go and save my child." Why is it that you won't enter and save your child? Because your life is dearer to you than your own child. Therefore, you do not venture into the building to rescue the child, because you do not want to lose yourself.

The reason is, you are dear to yourself. Therefore, the real source of happiness and joy is your own being and this joy is already there within you. In your essential nature, you are nothing but the embodiment of joy and happiness.

In your real nature, you are already bliss itself. In deep sleep, you do not experience any worldly things, nor do you experience the people around you, nor the universe, which has disappeared, nevertheless, you derive bliss.

Where has that bliss come from? People imagine that bliss or happiness comes from contact with the outside world. But in deep sleep, the world outside is not there. The things of the world are not there, the people around you are not there, and even the outside experiences are not there. But then where does the bliss come from in deep sleep? The bliss that you experience in deep sleep comes from your own Self, you own *Atman*. Your own *Atman*, in its own natural nature, is all bliss, just as much as the nature of the sun is heat and light, so also the true essential nature of the *Atman*, which is your essential nature, is nothing but bliss. Therefore, every night you are experiencing the bliss of the *Atman*. The only thing is, you are unconsciously experiencing it. If you can consciously experience it, that is called *Samadhi*, or enlightenment. That same bliss, gets experienced consciously, and knowingly in the state of enlightenment. Because you get enlightened to your own true state of blissful existence.

That is why before you go to sleep, you make all the elaborate preparations. In fact, when you go any place, the first thing you look for is a place to sleep. Because unconsciously, you want to experience that blissful repose which is so refreshing and soothing. It soothes your being. So if you can be in that state permanently, perpetually, but consciously, what a glorious and wonderful state of being would it be! To be in that state for all time is what is attained in enlightenment, and that is your Divine Nature. In your Divine Nature, when you experience your divinity, it is that bliss that you will be experiencing for all times.

Therefore, who is that man who would refuse to have that bliss? You can deprive a man of anything, but you cannot deprive him of one thing - sleep. Because that sleep is so desirable. It refreshes him and in it he enjoys the bliss of his own existence. It is the nature of his own being. Therefore, it is that bliss or happiness, which this person who has gone within in sleep is experiencing. But to obtain that consciously, there has to be a sacrifice.

Once again we come back to sacrifice. If you want to achieve or obtain anything in the world, some sacrifice has to be done. People in the world go through many sacrifices to obtain the things of the world; either to get a good job, or to make some money in the world. So too also in spiritual life, in order to attain your glorious ultimate state of being, a sacrifice has to be done. You must gradually realize the futility of the little pleasures and joys that you indulge in, and are addicted to, and are caught up with, and realize that it is high time to put an end to all these little fleeting pleasures. This is the sacrifice that you are enjoined upon so that by doing so you can subsequently derive the glorious bliss of the *Atman*. Thus should you make yourself competent.

This is that person who has gone within and is experiencing the bliss of the *Atman*. That is where his happiness is. And once obtained, is obtained forever. You will never lose it thereafter. Therefore, he says, "*Tasya kaaryam na vidyate.*" For such a person there is nothing to be done. For the whole purpose of life and living is to realize the Self. Since he has attained or realized what has to be realized. He is free and has gone beyond this world. It is a very unusual thing. You are attaining something, which was ever there ever present within. You are realizing something which is already there within you. It is not something which has to be brought in from the outside. The kingdom of heaven is within. You are already the Divine. So what you have to do now, is to realize the fact that - Thou art the Divine - and become conscious of it.

A beautiful example of this is the following story. There was a prince who took part in a drama. And in that particular drama, he played the part of a beggar. After the drama was over, the prince who was so identified and involved with his role as a beggar, still continued to play the part of a beggar even after the drama was over. He felt that he was a beggar and so went about the streets of the kingdom, lamenting to himself, as all beggars lament about, especially so in Eastern countries. He went around lamenting about his poor plight, and asking people for pennies. Because he had played the part of a beggar, he was in tattered rags. As he had identified himself so strongly, he forgot who he was and began feeling that he was a beggar.

In the meantime, the king had died, and the throne was waiting for him. It was now an embarrassment for the officials of the kingdom. So they came up to him and told him, "Look here, prince."

The prince said, "What prince? You know what I am. See my garb?"

So they said, "Well, you are not the beggar that you perceive yourself to be. You are really the prince of this kingdom. The king has passed away and the throne is waiting for you."

He just couldn't believe it, because his prior identification was so strong. But nevertheless, the ministers seemed to be so sober and well-mannered. They had long white beards. In all seriousness they were telling him that he was the prince of the kingdom, and that he was now the king. And they said, "Come, we will take you to your palace."

And since they were talking to him so politely and earnestly, he listened to them incredulously. The resistance to the initial disbelief began collapsing and he agreed to be led by them, trusting them and their words. They were even extra courteous to him, for the person who played the part of a beggar could very well play the part of a king, and could very well reprimand them for impolite behavior towards the king.

So naturally they were all very polite to him, and led him to the palace. When he was walking into the palace, in spite of his tattered garbs, all the guards and officials were saluting him. So that gave him a little more confidence. And then the officials told him, "The throne is there, go and sit down on it. It is there for you." And he sat there and began feeling the sweetness of the throne, and the fans too, were being waved by charming damsels. He thought, "Yes, perhaps I am the king," and had a good feeling about it. Thereafter he began playing the part of a king and realized, "I am the king, indeed!"

Exactly the same problem is here also. In your essential nature - thou art the Divine - the glorious Divine. On account of an error, you may call it an ignorance, you have become veiled, or covered from your true Self. As a result of it, you are now behaving like a human being, or rather, misbehaving as a human being to be more precise. So this is the part that you are playing now in the living drama of life. For the world is the stage and every man an actor playing his real life-like role totally focused and identified with his assigned part in the theatrical production wherein the actors are also the witness-audience, for whose benefit the play has been staged. But the players of the drama of life, blissfully unaware of this truth, have to be brought back to their senses. It is indeed ironical, the pun or the phrase, "to be brought back to one's senses," is possible in this instance, only when you lose contact with the "senses," and then only do you get back to your senses. It seems as if we have all lost our senses as to who we really are, and have to get back or recover our true sense of being.

Therefore, to effect this, somebody has to come and tell you that, "Thou art the Divine." And that somebody is the scripture. All the words of the wise, who have realized the truth, pronounce and affirm this truth. The Messiah - in this case Lord Krishna, is telling you that, "Thou art the Divine." He is saying it in so may words and explaining to you all about your divinity. Since Krishna is talking, there is sense in what he is saying. Although he talks often in riddles in a veiled language mixed with baffling humor, nevertheless at other times, he is all seriousness. Hence, Arjuna is compelled to believe what Krishna is saying with all reason and logic.

Gradually he becomes convinced of his Divine Nature. In the same way too, the scriptures first reveal to you your divine nature; then you believe and develop confidence and thereafter all that you have to do is, begin to feel and become aware of your Divine Nature. That is all that has to be done. The divinity is already there within you. You have forgotten it. Therefore the teaching tells you, "Thou art the Divine."

In the beginning, you are unable to accept it. It takes time to

102

be convinced of the fact of your Divine Nature. Because you begin to revolt, just like the prince who was playing the part of the beggar, you too refuse to accept the truth of it in the beginning. It takes time for the understanding to unfold. Thereafter, all that you have to do, is to become aware. That is exactly what is done in meditation. In meditation, all that you are trying to do is, once again become Self-aware. This leads to recognition.

So in meditation you are learning to recognize, (re-cognize). Thus the recognition is taking place, and that brings about the realization of your Divine Nature. Therefore, in such a context, there is no activity possible. For a person who has understood his own true nature, all that he has to do is, learn to re-cognize. Thus these great souls, once they have obtained the state of detachment, go into the jungles and monasteries, live a secluded, contemplative life and try to re-cognize. The recognition comes over a period of time, and eventually the experience takes place through the intense force of re-cognition. When the recognition takes place, that is called *Brahman* experience, or God-realization, in religious parlance. That is why for a man of God there is nothing to be done. No activity is basically possible for him. So says Krishna.

Then in the next verse (eighteen), he says:

****

नैव तस्य कृतेनार्थ: नाकृतेनेह कश्चन ।
न चास्य सर्वभूतेषु कश्चिदर्थव्यपाश्रय: ॥ १८ ॥

Naiva tasya kritenaartho naakriteneha kascana |
Na caasya sarva bhuteshu kaschidarthavyapaasrayaha ||

To him there is no interest in the doing, of anything, or in the not doing of anything.
Also he is not dependent on any being for anything. (18)

****

By doing anything, such an individual does not gain anything. Because he is full in nature of being and has already attained what has to be attained.

In the world, a person does many things to achieve whatever he wants and does many things to obtain it. But once you have realized your divinity, is there anything else to achieve? Can there be anything for you to do in the world? Once you have attained and realized your glorious state, all that you do thereafter is abide in it. You are now the king of kings, as Jesus was called, the king of kings.

Since he does not need anything, therefore, there is no need for him to get into any action at all. Since there are no desires to fulfill, nothing to achieve, no ambitions left, and nothing to accomplish in the world, no further activity is possible for him.

Also at the same time, he does not lose anything by not doing anything. Neither does he gain anything by doing anything. Now if you do not do anything, you lose a lot. If you do not go to work, first of all you lose your job and finally your wife as well. I once stayed with an American who was a senior engineer and an advisor in Houston. The company began to lay off. The first persons they began to lay off were the advisors because they are redundant. And then he was looking for a job for a long time in that area, and could not get one. He also told me, that if he does not get a job quickly, his wife would be leaving him. So when you lose something, and don't do something about it, you stand to lose many things as well. In America you lose your house, you lose your car, and your furniture, and finally lose your wife too, and everything. Therefore, by not doing anything, you stand to lose everything but this person does not lose anything.

In fact, by not doing what you are supposed to do, you incur a defect, called *pratyavaya dosha*. That is the defect of non-performance of duties. Every person has certain obligative duties and functions which he has to do and perform in the world. If perchance he does not do his duty, then by the virtue of not doing his duty, he incurs demerit, or *paapa*. That state of affairs is called *pratyavaya dosha*. Also if you don't do what you have to do, then later on, you will be made to do that same thing perhaps with interest. That is a law of life. Thus what you have not done, will have to be done subsequently with interest, too. But such a situation is not there for this person.

So by not doing anything, he does not lose anything as he has nothing to gain in the world, and also nothing to lose in the world, too. Because he is self-complete in his own being. By being what he is, he cannot lose himself. Thus he has nothing further to achieve or to lose in the world. Therefore, he has nothing to do and nothing not to do also.

Then at the same time, *na kaschidartha vyapaasrayaha*. This individual is not dependent upon anybody for anything. From the god *Brahma* down to the most minute creatures, he is not dependent for anything. He is totally free, totally independent, and totally unconcerned. There is absolutely nothing that he wants. He is self-content, and self-satisfied in his own essential nature as the Divine. Because the person who realizes the Divine is verily the Divine itself. Can the Divine want anything? Therefore, it is not dependent on anybody for anything in the whole universe.

Then as for the physical body, it gets taken care of as per its own *prarabda karma*. That is, every living creature gets born with its own system of maintenance. Because he knows as per the law of *karma*, the physical body gets taken care of. And even if it is not taken care of, he is not concerned as he has risen above body-consciousness. But people of the world are totally dependent on something or the other. Everyone is dependent on everybody else.

But this is the only person who is absolutely free and independent. Therefore, once you learn to live the life of a *sannyasi*, a renunciate monk, then only you learn to realize the charm of it. What an independent, totally free life it is, provided you are able to live like that. It is a free life meant to lead you to total freedom. You can go anywhere, be anywhere. You don't have to tell anybody where you are going, where you are coming, where you are staying. You can disappear anywhere you want.

And *sadhus* know this truth very well. So when a *sadhu - fakir-* has an *ashram* of his own, and leaves and goes away for awhile, it may be for a few days, a few months, or even for a few years. Or it may also be that he may not ever come back. He just goes away somewhere, never to return. As has nowhere to go, and nowhere to come, he is free to go anywhere. He is able to do this and be like this, as he has no attachment to anything or for anybody.

There was a *sannyasi*, who had gone to a particular village, and as he was leaving had indicated that he was going in that particular direction towards another village. Then all of a sudden, they found him going in the opposite direction, so they said to him, "We thought you were going in that direction."

He replied, "Yes, I was going in that direction, but the wind was blowing and my hair was falling into my eyes, so I turned directions and am going this way." So they have nowhere to go. *Sannyasis* are the last people that you can depend on. You never know where they will be going, and from where they will be coming.

As such in northern India, in the states of Punjab, Haryana, and Uttar Pradesh, simple cottages have been built by the people of the locality for such *sannyasis* -hermit monks- to come and stay. The door of the cottage is always left open because you never know from which corner the *sannyasi* will come and reside there for some time. At the same time, you never know when he will leave. One fine day you will find him not there. So their way of life is like that.

In India, sometimes those *sannyasis* travel by train. So they go to the railway station and get into the first train that comes by. You know where you have to go and all that is very clear to you. But he goes into the Indian railway station wherein there are half a dozen platforms with as many trains going in different directions. He gets into the first train that comes by, sits in it for some time, and then alights from it if he feels like getting down, on seeing some place that looks all right, and then just goes somewhere. That is how some of them keep on living.

In their unique way of living, they are not dependent on anybody for anything in the world. As free as a bird they go about living their lives. Theirs is a different life in a different world altogether. But Arjuna, as far as you are concerned, you are not like that. You are lamenting that, 'These are my people, I'll be killing them.' The moment you say, "My, my, my," you have responsibilities. Till when do you have responsibilities? So long as you feel that you have this "my" sense, so long do you have all the responsibilities. My husband, my wife, my children, my house, my everything. So long as you are prepared to use that word "my," all the responsibilities come unto you. It is the same thing here with Arjuna, too. He had used the word "my" people, and therefore he felt that he had all the responsibilities: and thus was concerned about his duties to one and all, and therefore was perplexed.

Hence in the next verse, Krishna says:

****

तस्मादसक्तस्सततं कार्यं कर्म समाचर ।
असक्तो ह्याचरन्कर्म परमाप्नोति पूरुषः ॥ १९ ॥

107

Tasmaathasaktaha satatam kaaryam karma samaacara |
Asakto hiyaacaran karma paramaapnoti puurushaha ||

Therefore without attachment, always do well obligative actions.
Performing actions indeed without attachment, men attained the highest
(reality).   (19)
****

'Arjuna, since you do not have the character of one
established in the Self, and this fact is evident to you, therefore, you
very well know that you have to get into this action which happens to
be your *dharma*, or duty in life. *Satatam kaaryam karma
samaachara.* That is, always perform well the function of life, which
you are supposed to do.'

Every person in life has certain duties and responsibilities
which he has to perform and discharge. What these functions are is
known to each and every one. You know what you have to do, and
what your enjoined actions are for the day. So do those actions
which you are supposed to do. When those actions come your way,
may you take those actions and perform them happily, and pleasantly.
This is the "art of living." Thus with a pleasant from of mind, knowing
what you have to do, get into action.

But then how should you do it? *Asaktaha* - without being
attached. Here it means, without being attached to the very actions,
be they pleasant or unpleasant. As both types of actions come one's
way in life. May you keep on doing all the functions and duties
without being attached either to the action, or to the results of action.
Thus the living of life should be gone through. Why is it so? For
what purpose? The reason why you have to do it without attachment
is: *"Asakto hi aacharan karma, param aapnoti puurusaha."*
Performing actions without attachment, man attains the highest reality.

How does that happen? By going through actions without

attachment to the action, or its results thereof, one gradually rises above action to the actionless state. When actions are done without desires for the fruits of action, then by virtue of that, one goes beyond desire too. Thus by performing what you have to do, by being action oriented and not result conscious, you get purified. As a result, you obtain *chitta sudhhi*, or the purity of mind. Once you have obtained the purity of mind, then this will help you to get established in the *Atman*, the Self. Purity of mind will help one to get into a state of meditation or the state of meditative awareness. Therefore, purity of mind is essential for a spiritual life.

An impure man, with a gross, crude, and a worldly mind, will find it very difficult to get into the state of meditation. His mind is heavy with gross worldly impressions and thoughts. Such a mind has to become subtle and refined. When it is purged of its worldly patterns and thoughts, then that mind becomes pure and will attain the capacity to maintain the meditative state. In the meditative state one tends to become aware of one's own Divine Nature. It is the process of becoming re-aware of one's divinity. Thus by re-cognition, recognition takes place. Hence through meditation the experience of one's glorious state of divinity transpires.

Therefore, every person living in the world, should go through his normal worldly duties, without attachment and perform his functions as a *yagna*, that is, as a sacrifice. By virtue of that, he obtains *chitta sudhi*, or mental purification which facilitates an inner contemplative life.

In the next two verses, Krishna is giving an example of great personalities who were householders, who had attained this Blessed Divine State. When you know that people who were like you had lived an active life in the world and had attained the Blessed State through action, so could you too. This fact inspires you to go through your actions and lead an active contemplative life while living in the world.

So here the beautiful example is:

****

कर्मणैव हि संसिद्धिमास्थिता जनकादयः ।
लोकसंग्रहमेवापि संपश्यन्कर्तुमर्हसि ॥ २० ॥

Karmanaiva hi samsiddhimaasthita janakaadayaha |
Lokasamgrahamevaapi sampasyan kartumarhasi ||

Janaka and others attained to the state of perfection only by action.
Even by keeping-in-view the welfare of the world only, you should
do action.   (20)

****

King Janaka, is the example given here. So he says,
"*Karmana eva hi samsiddhim asthitha janakaadaya.*" King
Janaka, and other kings too, attained to the state of perfection only
through action. They did not give up action, but went through their
daily obligative functions and eventually attained to the state of
perfection.

What were the actions they did? As Janaka was a king, he
ruled a kingdom. While governing a kingdom, he attained to this
glorious God state. He ruled the kingdom as a *yagna*, a sacrifice.
He ruled the kingdom, which was his function, and daily obligative
duty. But he ruled it as a *karma yogi*. As a *yoga* of action, he ruled
the kingdom, and thereby obtained mental purification, and thereafter
realized his own true nature as the Divine.

Thus the great King Janaka, had done action before and
attained the highest. So too, many other kings like Ajaatasatru, etc.
attained the sublime state. Hence we find a spiritual tradition of holy

kings, referred to as *Raja Rishis*, who were the torch-bearers of this sacred spiritual knowledge leading to Enlightenment. In fact it is easier for kings to become hermits and to realize their divinity, because the kings have known life. They have experienced the good things of life. Hence dispassion or the state of *vairagya* comes easier for them, as they have had everything. Only when you have had your fill of life, do you become tired of it, and the world loses its charm. This is the fore-runner of dispassion. But for a person who hasn't seen life, dispassion is very difficult. That is why we find many a king and emperor of India, become men of God. Lord Buddha was such a classic example of a Prince attaining the Blessed state of *Nirvana*.

And even recently too, there was a good example of a man of action. He was not a king, but an ordinary betel-leaf seller. He was selling betel-leaves, of all cities, in the city of Bombay. In the busy metropolis of Bombay, he had a small shop. And these betel-leaf shops are very small in India and are hardly a four foot by four foot cubicle. In that little shop, he made his livelihood, and maintained his family. That was his occupation. But he converted his occupation into a spiritual discipline and became a *Brahma-jhani*, that is, a man of God. From the very heart of the metropolitan city of Bombay, he went through his *karmas*, that is, his actions and functions as a *yoga*, and attained that supreme immortal state.

Here also we find an example, that these great kings in the ancient days in India, went through their actions as a *yoga*. Their obligative function was to go through ruling a kingdom. You too, have your own functions in your own way, just as the king had his own function of ruling a kingdom.

It is said of Janaka, that even though he was a king, he was going through his scriptural studies too from his teacher. Regular classes were taking place in the palace. The king had also permitted a few *Brahmacharis* - religious novitiates, who were fellow students, to live in the palace. They were given quarters in one wing at the outskirts of the palace. As they were *Brahmacharis*, spiritual-minded novitiates, their possessions were very few.

So as usual, the classes go on. Janaka is a very busy person as he is the ruler of a kingdom. Therefore, he is very busy and comes right on time for the class. Sometimes circumstances compel him to come late too. As such, till he comes, the teacher does not begin the classes. So the other disciples thought to themselves, "Our *guru*, is being partial to Janaka because he is the king." They did not realize that the partiality was shown because Janaka was the best student. Therefore, they were a little upset about it. And the *guru* knew that these people were a little dissatisfied over this issue. So he waited for an opportunity when he could explain the situation to them.

One day, as the class was going on, the palace messengers came there and told the king that, "The palace is on fire." The king heard it, and dismissed the messengers. Now the moment the other fellow students heard that the palace was on fire, bolted from the class then and there, to go and retrieve their articles in the palace. While the king who had the opportunity to lose the entire palace, was seated there quietly listening to the discourse.

So when they came back, they found the king still seated there, and the *guru* had a hearty laugh at the whole episode. Then they realized their own foolishness. Because even though Janaka was a king, he was detached, he didn't have attachment. So what if the palace goes? It is only a palace made of brick and mortar. A king doesn't cease to be a king by virtue of the loss of a palace. He is still a king. Also he knew that there were others who would take care of the whole incident. But the idea is, there was detachment in him. Hence without attachment, he was able to rule the kingdom. Anxiety-free fearlessness was there in him. That is the character you too need in living life.

In the same manner, too, whatever you do in the world, and whatever responsibilities you have, take care of them with an anxiety-free, detached frame of mind. Then you are a success in living life. Thus take care of your children too, as a trust. As a trustee they have been entrusted to you in this life and to the best of your abilities, take care of the children according to their own innate talents. By that you have done the best you could, and your duty is over. But then, you don't want to stop at that. You want to take care of their children, too. That is where the whole problem of attachment comes in. Because of attachment, there is anxiety in taking care of the children. Therefore, without attachment, do everything and go about doing everything that you have to do in life. It is in this sense that one has to go about leading one's life.

Then he says further, 'There is another reason, too, why you should get into this action, which is your duty.' "*Lokasamgraham eva api sampusyan kartum arhasi.*" 'That is, for the good of the world, you should do action.' *Lokasamgaraha* means doing good to the world. Every person in some way or the other, feels like doing some good in the world in some form or the other. Thus depending on what situation you are in, according to your situation, station and position in life, you very well know in what way you can contribute your might to the welfare and to the good of the world around you. That is a natural tendency.

'Arjuna, you are a responsible person, a prince participating in the ruling of the kingdom. Therefore, your responsibility is very great here. Considering the welfare of the world, in checking evil and injustice, you will have to get into this action. It is your duty to protect the kingdom, to uproot unrighteousness, and establish justice. That is your duty. If you do not do your duty, then unrighteousness would prevail in the world around you. Therefore, you are duty-bound to do what you have to do here, and set an example to the world. If responsible people do not come forward and do what they have to do, what can other people do, when there is unrighteousness prevailing? Therefore, you are duty-bound to get into this war, which is part of the overall battle-of-life.'

Verses 21 - 26

Verse 21:

****

यद्यदाचरति श्रेष्ठस्तत्तदेवेतरो जनः ।
स यत्प्रमाणं कुरुते लोकस्तदनुवर्तते ॥ २१ ॥

Yatyadaacarati srestastatadevataro janaha |
Sa yatpramaanam kurute lokastadanuvartate ॥

Whatsoever the exalted do, that the other people also do;
Whatever he sets up as the standard, that the world follows. (21)

****

Lord Krishna is adducing further reasons why Arjuna should get into this action of war, which happened to be his obligative function or duty in life. He said in the previous verse that even for the welfare of the world, one has to go through certain actions and deeds which will be of use for the collective good. It is especially so in the case wherein unrighteousness prevails, and one has to overcome it and establish *dharma* or righteousness. Perhaps in order to do that, one may have to remove it lock, stock, and barrel, that is completely, even by the ultimate means available, in this instance a war.

Having said that much, he says, 'You as an elder in society, have to set an example. For whatever the elders do, the others emulate. And being a prince, a member of the ruling royal family, you have to set high standards.' Therefore, whatever the rulers do is always followed by the subjects.

That is why he is saying, "*Yat yat aacharati srestras tat ta eva etaro janah.*" Whatever the elders and leaders of society do, that indeed the common people follow. If a fashion is set in vogue by a very popular person in any field in society, immediately all the rest follow that trend.

115

About sixty years ago in England, the Prince of Wales at that time, set a hat fashion in vogue by wearing a particular type of top-hat. It was said that the whole of London was filled with top-hats moving about, because that was the fashion set in vogue. So whether it be a good fashion, a good or a bad example, set by the elders, is naturally followed by the others. Therefore, people in responsibility should realize that they become an example to others and thereby ought to conduct their life with a sense of responsibility.

When Mahatma Ghandi set an austere pattern of living in India during the pre-independence days, a good many of the leaders also similarly emulated whatever he did. They dressed in a simple manner and in due course even the Ghandi cap came into popular vogue. Though Gandhi himself never wore a cap, nevertheless the cap signified simplicity. Even in homes too, whatever the mother wears, the daughters want to wear too.

Thus he says, 'The conduct, and the type of action maintained by you as an elder in society becomes the authority for the common people around, and they naturally tend to follow suit.' For people ape and follow what the others do. "*Yat pramaanam kurute, lokah tad anuvartate.*" Whatever standard is set by the elders, that the people tend to follow as an authority.

Therefore, when one is in a position of authority, one has to live very carefully in the world, so as to set an example in the society around. 'Therefore, Arjuna, in this instance, you have now come here to take part in a righteous war, and establish righteousness in the land, and prevail over evil. And if perchance, you are not going to do what you are supposed to do, then the others too, in the society, would follow you and they would also not do what they are supposed to do.' Thus evil and unrighteousness would prevail in the land. This would be tragic for all concerned.

The question arises as to whether any war is righteous. War by itself is not desirable. But the human animal creates conditions for war impelled by its animal nature. When a race or a nation of people have been deprived of their rights, their right to live, their right to land, and have been forcibly deprived of their possessions, then a war-like situation is being created.

Thus it is unrighteous to deprive people of their land, and their possessions by force. By that an unrighteous war has been declared upon a race or a nation of people who are living peacefully. Thereafter for the victims to reclaim their right to land and their right to live peacefully, becomes a righteous war.

It was unrighteous for Hitler to have invaded the rest of Europe, and to have had various nations under its subjugation. Thereafter for the rest of the world to get together and fight back Hitler to regain their land, was righteous.

Even within a nation, when one race sends its armed forces to conquer and overpower another race of people living peacefully within its own country, and deprive them of their right to land, and their right to live peacefully, then an unrighteous war has been declared by the State upon a minority race within its own nation. Then it becomes righteous for the victim race to fight back the State and reclaim its right to land and its right to live peacefully.

We see this phenomenon of "ethnic cleansing" of the minority race by the majority race in State-sponsored terrorism and brute armed force occurring even today in certain nations. In such a situation, the victim race has no other recourse left, except to either perish or fight back the State and obtain its right to live with honour and dignity. Then it becomes a righteous war for the victim race, to fight back the evil of the State.

It was a similar situation here in the Mahabharata episode,

wherein Arjuna and the Pandavas were deprived of their rights, their right to land, and their right to their kingdom. All peaceful recourse towards an amicable settlement failed, war was the only recourse left to regain their deprived rights. Thus such a war becomes a righteous war, a dharma yuddha, so says Krishna in verses 31 and 33 of the second chapter of the Gita. Therein he makes reference to the term "righteous war" - *dharmiyam samgraamam*, or "*dharmiyaat yuddhat.*"

In fact a state or a nation which has evil designs upon another race or a nation, will never listen to reason, nor want a settlement, but go through its evil design of the annihilation of the other race or nation, unless it is otherwise checked. Here too, Dhuryodana refused to listen to reason, nor want a settlement, but opted for war to complete his evil design of annihilating Arjuna and the Pandavas.

Then he gave himself as an example. In the next three verses, Lord Krishna says:

****

न मे पार्थास्ति कर्तव्यं त्रिषु लोकेषु किञ्चन ।
नानवाप्तमवाप्तव्यं वर्त एव च कर्मणि ॥ २२ ॥

Na me paarthaasti kartavyam trisu lokasu kinchana |
Naanavaaptamavaaptavyam varta eva ca karmani ||

There is nothing in the three worlds which should be done by me oh Partha; nor is there anything unattained which should be attained; yet I engage in action.   (22)

****

Herein the word Paarta stands for Arjuna, because he comes from the dynasty of the Prita family. 'Oh scion of the Pritas, may you understand, that as far as I am concerned, *na me thrisu lokaasu kinchana kartavyam* - in the three worlds, I have nothing whatsoever to do.' Why is it that the Lord has nothing to do in the three worlds? Because the Divine is self-complete in its own existence. It is absolute fullness, and is perfect and complete in its own being. That individual who is in want, gets into action to fulfill those wants. But the Divine has no needs and wants. Therefore, there is no need for the Divine to get into any action whatsoever in the three worlds.

Then what are the three worlds? Of course, the earth plane is one world, but there are two other worlds too. They are: the intermediate and the heavenly regions. Thus there are two types of heavens. There is one where you go and then come back, as you have earned your holiday through merit or *punya* earned here on Earth. You go to the intermediate heavenly regions to experience or enjoy the merits you have earned on the earth plane. After having experienced them, you come back. This is the heaven of returns.

Then there is the other heaven which is called the heaven-of-no-returns. In that heavens, you keep on living there along with Brahma, the Creator until the world's end, and thereafter get liberated, along with the gods living there. This is called gradual liberation. It is this type of heaven-of-no-returns, which the Christians talk about. They don't have the fine classification of the two types of heavens.

But the state of the Divine is beyond the heavens too. The nature of being of the Divine is beyond the heavens, wherein there are no regions, no worlds. In that transcendental state of enlightened being, there are no planes, or worlds. For all the worlds are in this universe, which is empirical in nature. That is, momentary and in time. But once you get enlightened, you transcend this empirical universe.

Therefore, Lord Krishna says, 'I have nothing to gain, or accomplish in any one of the three worlds. Nevertheless, I keep on going through various actions.' *"Na me karthavyam trisu lokasu kinchana asti."* 'I have nothing to do in the three world, yet I keep on doing whatever has to be done as the Creator.'

'As the Creator it is my function to create the universe, and then to take care of it, in all its minute detail.' The universe is not a chaos, but a remarkable cosmos. So being a cosmos, it requires a super-intelligent principle to keep an overall eye on the functioning of the universe. Therefore, there is immense activity being undertaken by the Creator, in taking care of the rhythm of the pulsative universe.

"Na anavaaptam avaaptavyam." 'There isn't anything unattained which I have to attain. As far as you ordinary mortals are concerned, you have to do something, because you have not attained what has to be attained. There are many things which you have to attain in life. In order to attain them and accomplish it, you have to get into action. But as far as I am concerned as the Divine, (Lord Krishna says), there isn't anything which is unattained which I have to attain. Because I am self-accomplished, I am complete and full. So there is nothing left for me to obtain in this world, or any one of the worlds. Nevertheless, I go about in the world, performing various actions.'

Lord Krishna is the *avatar*, the messiah, of the Creator. In the life of Lord Krishna as the messiah, he has duties and functions to do. From the moment he was born, he was busy getting into trouble and mischief. He was totally involved in some form of activity or the other. All through his life, someone or the other was trying to trouble him. He wanted to live peacefully, the way you want to live quietly and be at peace, but others don't allow you to keep quiet. Even from the moment he was born his life was at stake. There was a royal order for his execution. At least you are lucky, that your head was not harassed when you were born. But this poor Krishna's head was involved at that time. His poor mother was locked up in jail. His life was not to be spared, even before he was born. Just imagine his fate. He had to escape from all that and get away from all difficulties. And when he was a little child, Pudana, the wicked demon woman was sent to finish him.

Thereafter, he had to go through many battles with those who were intent on killing him. So all through his life he was harassed. Nevertheless, he never gave up hope. He was full of enthusiasm and vitality. For him, life was a *tamaasha*, a playful sport. But there was one little difference between his *tamaasha* and your *tamaasha*. His *tamaasha* was like play for him. Playfully he did everything in all seriousness, he engaged. He never lost sight of that seriousness. Seriously, he was playing about in the world. "Work is play, and play is work," was his motto of life. There was always that flick of a smile on his face. With a sense of humor, he was going about life. But if you asked somebody in India how his life is, with a sense of reluctance he will say, "*Chalta hai*," that is, "Just getting along." That is a typical answer given in India. Because people feel living life is a burden. But it is not to be understood so. The enitre burden is in the mind.

Thus, here was the example of a man living life with enthusiasm and vitality. With all interest he was living dynamically in the world, discharging all duties and functions. Where there was trouble, Krishna was there to take care of the situation. Of course, he created the problems, but he was there to solve them too. He was in the thick of all battles, and incidents. In every nook and corner his presence was felt.

That is why at the end of the Mahabharata war, when Ghaandaari went about the battleground, weeping over her dead sons, and finally saw the body of Abimanyu, who was the heir to the entire dynasty, she was overwhelmed with grief, even though he was not her direct grandson. Nevertheless, the entire clan cherished him, as the heir to the kingdom. And as she found him lying dead in the battlefield, she couldn't help herself, and burst out in tears. Then at that time, Krishna happened to pass by, or perhaps he knowingly passed that way. The moment she saw him, said, "Why did you do this? Why did you cause this?" She accused him of having brought about this entire havoc, of being responsible for all things that happen.

There was Krishna the controller of this universe. Like holding the reins of the horses, he was holding he reins of the universe. He played the part of a charioteer, playing a double role. One as a charioteer, and the other as a messiah. Even though to one side he had given away his own armies, to the other side, he was a charioteer controlling the destiny of the war. As the charioteer, which was symbolic, he was controlling the way the war was being fought.

And of course in his younger days, he took to his heels too. That is how he established the kingdom of Dwaaraka. He and his kinsmen were harassed so much by Kamsa and others, that they had a successful retreat, and went to Dwaaraka to live. It was a successful retreat. As Winston Churchill said, when they lost the initial battle in Dunkirk, "We have not lost the war, it is only a successful retreat, so that we can regroup together, arm ourselves and come back." Here is the same situation with Krishna. Playfully he amassed all the people and went over to Dwaaraka, only to come back with a mightier force to once again do battle with Kamsa and Shisupaala.

Therefore, you would find in the entire Mahabharata episode, Lord Krishna going about everywhere actively functioning. Wherever there was trouble, Krishna was there. Or you could say, where Krishna was, there was trouble. In some form or the other, his hand would be there. So he was actively involved, even though he had nothing to do.

There was the Rama *avatar* too. Rama came into the world,

in order to establish and show the people what righteous life is. For that he had to undergo much privation and difficulties. Had to endure much sorrow and misery, as he had to behave as a *mariyaata purushottam*. That is, as the person who was to set an example to fellow man, as to how to live *dharma*. So whatever *dharma* he sets, the others tend to follow. In the Ramayana episode, Rama himself had to live his life, setting it as an example, indicating how life is full of hardship and difficulty. So here also he says, "There isn't anything for me to achieve in the world. Nevertheless, I go about my own ways, doing what I have to do."

Then he says in the twenty-third verse:

****

यदि ह्यहं न वर्तेयं जातु कर्मण्यतन्द्रितः ।
मम वर्त्मांनुवर्तन्ते मनुष्याः पार्थ सर्वशः ॥ २३ ॥

Yadi hyaham na varteya jaadu karmanyatantritaha |
Mama varthmaanuvartante manusyaaha paarta sarvasaha ||

In case I do not get into action unwearied, people would follow my ways in all matters.   (23)

****

All people would follow my way, if I were to relax and take things easy. The people around me too, would be taking things easy. If Krishna is dynamic, then everybody is dynamic. Mahatma Ghandi's life in his *ashram* was so dynamic that everyone had to be on their toes in a dynamic manner. He never allowed respite for anybody. So here Krishna set an example and everyone had to follow it.

If perchance you get tired of what you have to do, then unconsciously you set yourself as an example for others to emulate and follow. They will also begin following your example of relaxing and taking things casually. And once everybody begins to relax, then everything collapses. When there is total relaxation, even to maintain life is not possible. Thus everybody is kept on their toes, in some form or the other, so that the mind will be active, vigilant and sharp. The moment you begin to relax, your body relaxes and so does your mind, too, and you begin to take things easy. When you begin to take things easy, the best in you does not come out. The best in a person comes out when a person is under pressure or when a person is constantly kept busy.

Normally what happens is, you are pushed to excellence by other people. But life itself is pushing you into excellence, so that the best in you can come out. This life is meant for action, therefore, in order to live life, we have to live fully and completely, and bring about excellence in all ways that we can. The moment we tend to relax, then dullness overpowers and laziness sets in. When dullness and laziness overpower you, the best in you cannot come out. Therefore, everybody has to be constantly on their toes, doing something or the other.

Of course, people get tired of work too. That is why they are given the two-day holiday so that they can recoup and go back for the next five days. Life is meant for that purpose. You go to work for five days, relax for two days, and then you are ready for the next five days. Thus life goes on. That is how life is to be lived. If you were to be relaxed for all seven days, you would be tired of living life. But on the other hand, if you are up on your toes for all seven days, then your whole life is a dynamic expression of living, and the best in you comes out to your satisfaction.

Therefore, Krishna says, 'All the time I am busy doing something or the other, and go about doing everything that has to be done.'

****

उत्सीदेयुरिमे लोकाः न कुर्यां कर्म चेदहम् ।
सङ्करस्य च कर्ता स्यामुपहन्यामिमाः प्रजाः ॥ २४ ॥

Utseedheyurime lokaa na kuryaam karma chedhaham |
Samkarasya ca kartaa syaamupahanyaamimaaha prajaaha ||

In case I do not do action, I would be destroying these people, and
cause the admixture or confusion of *dharma* and lead the people
into a bad state.   (24)

****

'In case I do not do these actions which I am supposed to
do, then these worlds would perish. I am the ruler of this universe,
the overlord who oversees the entire universe, and look into all things
which are happening. Therefore, I have to see that the universe is in
its cosmic rhythm. Furthermore, as the Incarnate in this life, as
Krishna, it is my duty to do whatever I have to do in this world, and
teach the people, both by my life, and by my teaching as well. I have
to reveal many truths to people. Thus I am constantly on my toes
doing many things in the world, and resolving many a crisis here and
there. At the same time I have to go about giving the teachings too.'
Krishna's whole life was a lesson in the art of living. The whole of
his life was so actively and dynamically lived. Yet, at the same time
he lived his life with a smile on his lips. Always there was a smile on
the face of Lord Krishna.

So in the world, everything goes in its own cosmic rhythm.
When the king is in court, all the ministers and people in the court are
all up on their toes. The moment the king is out of the court, everyone
relaxes. And when the king enters, everyone is at attention. Similarly
here also, in order to see that the entire universe is kept on its toes,
Krishna has to be at attention, and be alert to everything. He cannot

afford to relax or take it easy. Because if he does, then others do similarly. Therefore, he has to be on his toes all the time, observing everything everywhere.

'My life itself is to be a life meant for *dharma*. If I did not set this example in the world, then what would happen is *samkarasya karta siyam*. I would bring about confusion.' *Samkara* means confusion. In many of the other translations you find that the word *samkarasya* is coupled here with the word *varna*, (caste), which means the admixture of the castes. The admixture of the caste system. That is the explanation given in many of the traditional commentaries, interpretations, and translations too. But the *word varna*, caste, is an unnecessary addition to the word *samkarasya*. Here we find Krishna has only used the word *samkarasya* to mean, confusion at all levels of *dharma* and not in the sense of the admixture of the caste system.

As admixture of the so-called caste system is never possible, as no one in the world is a member of a caste by birth. Only so by *guna* and *karma*. That is, by nature (tendencies) and action, vide Gita 4-13. Thus meant to imply that it is a psychological system.

For a person who is truly a *Brahmin* will have dispassion for things mundane and will be focused totally towards god (*para Brahman*) only, and will never undertake either the worship of the pagan Hindu gods or perform any rituals. For, by nature and disposition, a true *Brahmana* would be incapable of both. Vide "Brihadaranyaka Upanishad," 3-5 and 4-4-21 and "Vajrasuchi Upanishad," which reveal who a true Brahmana is.

Hence the word *samkarasya* here stands for the admixture of duties and functions. People would be confused as to what to do, and what not to do, and thereby be functioning in a wrong manner, violating all norms of human decency and *dharma*.

The following is a good example of what happens. A man and a woman are living in a house with their children. The family is well-off at the moment. But the man is without a job. Since they are well-off for the time being, they may have inherited some fortune, and the man is squandering his fortune. The man is taking life easy and is very casual in his ways. He has nothing in particular to do in the world. So he is taking life very easy and casually, getting whatever he wants whenever he want, getting up whenever he wants, and going out whenever he want. The mother is also like that. Then what do you think of the children in the house? They don't have any motivation. They will not have a direct interest to do anything or achieve anything in the world. And they too, naturally, will take life easy in a relaxed manner. Because the parents are leading such an uninspired way of living. Naturally there will be a confusion in the mind of the children as to what is life.

Therefore there will be a confusion brought about in the minds of the children as to how to go about living life. As they see the people around them, busy and going about in their own ways. But they see their own parents take life so casually. Thus these children will not know what to do with themselves. So there will be uncertainty in their lives.

On the other hand, when the father has a way of life, and the mother has her way of living also, the children observe that. They realize that there is a purpose in living, and that their parents are going about life in their own rhythmic manner. Therefore, these children also will fall into a particular groove or pattern. Confusion would not be there. They would see how their parents are going about living, and that others are also going about living in the same manner.

If the elders of the society do not go about their right way of living, and if everybody takes it easy and light, it will create confusion in the society. When people do not do what they are supposed to do, then there is chaos, and then naturally confusion prevails in society. People do not know what to do and what not to do and how to go about their lives.

"*Sankarasya karta syamupahanyamimaaha prajaaha.*" 'By virtue of not doing what I am supposed to do, I would not only create confusion in the minds and lives of the people, but at the same time by that, bring about their destruction too.' The destruction of the people would occur by permitting and encouraging them to lead a very casual life. Life is not meant to be lived in a casual manner. That is death, but life is to be lived in a very purposeful way. When it is not lived purposefully, then one neither derives any sense nor joy in living life. Therefore by not giving a sense and a direction to the living of life, he would bring about the destruction of these people.

Lord Krishna further says, you as an elder of society, should act a little more wisely. Thus he says in verse 25:

****

सक्ताः कर्मण्यविद्वांसो यथा कुर्वन्ति भारत ।
कुर्याद्विद्वांस्तथासक्तश्चिकीर्षुर्लोकसङ्ग्रहम् ॥ २५ ॥

Saktaaha karmanyavidvaamso yathaa kurvanti bhaarata |
Kuryadvidvaamstathaasaktascikiirshulokasamgraham ||

O Bharata, just as the ignorant do action, attached to it, so too the wise do action without being attached, wishing the welfare of the world. (25)

****

Just as the ignorant people go about doing their actions with attachment, you should also go about doing actions but without attachment. The ignorant go about various actions and functions, attached to the results of action, as they want to reap the fruits thereof.

That is how the ignorant man functions. But the wise who have this knowledge, should go about doing actions with a sense of non-attachment.

Vidvaan, the knowledgeable person, refers to one who has not only the knowledge of the Atman, the absolute reality, but also the knowledge of *karma yoga*. This is opposed to the *avidvaan* ignorant, who neither has this knowledge of *karma yoga*, nor the knowledge of the Atman. For the knowledge of both is necessary for the effective performance of action as a *yoga* of action - *karma yoga*.

So this person who is knowledgeable should go about doing actions, which an ignorant man also does, but without being attached either to those actions, or to the results of those actions. Neither should he be motivated towards those actions induced by the results thereof. But goes through actions for the good of the world. *Lokasamgrahaartham*. He does the actions for the welfare of the world, and to set an example and teach them. Hence a true *karma yogi* is a knowledgeable person.

Therefore, he is telling Arjuna, 'You are now to go through this action as you have now become a knowledgeable person.' But do, what you have to do, without being motivated by its outcome. The ignorant person is getting into action because he wants the result of it, or because he wants to please other people. But here, you are going to do it because it has to be done. You are duty-bound to do it. With that the action is over.

Also the ignorant man will go through his actions with anxiety for the results. When there is anxiety over the results, then there would be anxiety in the very performance of action itself. Thus an ignorant man will go through actions with anxiety. A series of actions go to make the living of life. Therefore, when a man goes through life with anxiety, he is also living life with anxiety.

The living of life is not separate from actions. Thus with anxiety he lives through his life with a feeling, "Will I get this, or not? Will I achieve or not? Will I be frustrated with this action or not? Will there be success in this venture, or will there be a failure?" In this manner there is always an anxiety and an unease.

How do you get over it? Do not be concerned with the results of actions, but do, what you have to do, with the best of your ability. The result naturally will be the best it could be. Let it turn out any way. According to the laws of life, let the results turn out the way they are meant to be. That is not in your hands. If it is a success, so be it. If it is a failure, so be it. Accept that too. That is what Lord Krishna showed us with his life.

Do you think there was any reason or need for Lord Krishna to retreat to Dwaaraka? After all, he is the incarnate himself, with all powers. No, he had to show people that life is a combination of both successes and failures. Often in the world, we have to retreat, too. Thus when you are able to go through life without this anxiety for the results of actions, then automatically, the actions are gone through in a very calm manner. This calm state is the sine-quo-non, the very essence of *karma yoga* or the living of life.

Very often, when people sit for an examination, they have anxiety. They are very nervous about whether they will do well in the exam or not, whether they will pass or not. But it would be better if a person would say, all right I am going to sit down quietly and do the best that I can. Sit down, do it, and then come out. In the world, too, life has to be gone through in such a manner.

Therefore, the ignorant person is going through life with anxiety, and performing actions too, with anxiety. But when the wise perform these actions in a calm and serene manner, then other people begin to observe this. What has brought about this calmness and serenity? After all, both are doing the same thing. There is only one difference. It is that enlightened understanding, that wisdom. It is that wisdom that has brought about this change in the individual. Therefore, in a very subtle manner, one would be able to perceive the calmness and the serenity of the knowledgeable person.

Therefore, the knowledgeable person goes about doing actions in the world, without undue concern for the fruits of actions, and without egoism. He does it for the welfare of the world.

At the same time, what else would he do?

****

न बुद्धिभेदं जनयेदज्ञानां कर्मसङ्गिनाम् ।
जोषयेत्सर्वकर्माणि विद्वान्युक्तःसमाचरन् ॥ २६ ॥

Na buddhibhedam janayedajnaanaam Karmasanghinaam |
Jyoshayetsarvakarmaani vidvanyuktaha samaacaran ||

The wise should not generate confusion of thought in the mind of the ignorant who are attached to action;
Being established in *yoga* he should engage them in all actions, himself performing them well.   (26)

****

That teacher who teaches wisely, will not create confusion and misunderstanding in the minds of the students. He only teaches as much as the students can comprehend. Beyond that, they don't teach. Jesus was such an example of a good teacher.

Once I had a very interesting experience in Florida. It was a group discussion for a group of Americans, and there were two women amongst them who were talking as if they were too knowledgeable. I was giving explanations to the others. But on a certain topic, I didn't give an answer and explain to them. Then there was another American woman who understood why I did not give them the answer. She told the other two women, "Of what use is it to you if he tells you this? You won't be able to live by it. Therefore, he is not telling you, he is keeping quiet." So you only teach as much as the others can appreciate and understand. Any other knowledge than that becomes futile.

"Na buddhibhetam janayet ajnanam karma sanghinam." One must not disturb the minds of the ignorant who are attached to action. A knowledgeable person, is one who has a knowledge of *karma yoga*, and also the knowledge of the *Atman*, the ultimate reality. Thus the knowledgeable person should not disturb the minds of ignorant people who are attached to action. If you were to disturb them, they would neither do their actions, nor would they be able to rise to your level of understanding and live by it. Therefore, you should not disturb their minds. But in a gentle manner, when the occasion arises, the correction is made. You wait for the time. A parent knows well, when their child requires a correction and they wait for the right time and the opportunity, to give that corrective advice in a gentle manner. Here also, the knowledgeable person should not disturb the minds of the ignorant, but give them a knowledge and an understanding that would not confuse them, nor would deter them from what they are supposed to do.

Otherwise an ignorant person will take the advice literally, if you tell them that the *Atman* is actionlessness, and that there is nothing for the *Atman* to do. If he is told that as the *Atman*, the Blessed Divine, they are ever full, and have nothing to do in this world, he will take your advice very literally. He will say, "I have been told that I am the *Atman*, that I am ever full, that there is nothing further for me to do, but to keep quiet and do nothing." One must be careful in giving the teaching. It should be taught in such a way, that the implication of the knowledge should be understood. An ignorant person who is reluctant to act should only be given that much teaching which would enable him to get into action. A person who is reluctant to get into action should not be told right away to function in the world with a detached perspective, as the man is still lethargic, and sluggish to get into action. Such a person should first be instigated into action with the accruing benefits thereof.

After the man has experienced the benefit of action and has the enthusiasm for action, then it is time for the stage two of the teaching. Now tell him, there is a better way of doing this action with a detached perspective. For, the detached way of doing things, takes the tension out of the living of life, and enables one to live peacefully. Thereafter, gradually set an example, and impel him towards action which is to be done as a *yoga* of action.

"*Vidvan yuktaha samaachara.*" So the wise established in yoga should perform actions well. No action should be left incomplete, but be done to its conclusion. Do it well, and while doing it, do those actions in a peaceful and calm manner, without any excitement. When you are able to go through action in this manner with equipoise and equanimity, then this mental state of serenity, is said to be the state of *yoga*. This is a definition for *yoga* in the Gita.

If you are able to go through actions in a very serene and calm manner, without being attached to the very action or the results of action, or without any anxiety, then the other person observes the way you are doing actions, and he too emulates and follows accordingly. Thus you not only do the actions, but also make the other person do actions. Hence, 'Arjuna, you too should get into this battle, which is your duty and thereby inspire others to go through their respective duties in life.'

From the next verse onward, there is a different line of thought altogether. It is said to be the science of action. It is totally a different concept altogether. What is that factor which causes action in you.?

What is that because of which you feel that you are the "doer" and the enjoyer? If you were to know those factors which bring about all activity and action in the universe, then you will come to realize, that in a real sense, you are not the doer. Actions are not done by you, but they are being done. They become operative. The rain rains, the sun shines, the flood waters move, the tree grows, the mind thinks. Everything has its own natural activity.

What is that factor that brings about these activities? If these factors are understood, then you will come to realize, that in a real sense you are not the doer of any activity. You come to realize that all actions are being done. The hands keep on moving, the tongue talks, the mind thinks, and everything goes on and is being done.

Thereafter, you will be able to appreciate your real nature as the non-doer, the non-performer. Even though actions are being done, you will come to realize that you are not the doer. When you come to realize that you are not the doer, by virtue of that you get absolved of all actions which go through you. Neither are you responsible for the meritorious, nor for the non-meritorious actions. You know that the actions are being done and gone through as a natural process, and you have nothing to do with it. Therefore in case Arjuna takes part in this battle, and does what he is supposed to do, he gets absolved of all actions, as he is not the doer.

The next few verses bring about this enlightened understanding. They are very important as they bring out its practical application into life. The practical application of anything always requires its theoretical foundation. They go together. The theoretical knowledge will help you to bring about its practical application. Theory and its application go together, and it is mentioned together in the Bhagavad Gita and in the Upanishads.

Verses 27 - 29

Lord Krishna was saying that one should act in the world, and go through one's actions without attachment. But then, people get into various activities being attached to the very action itself. What causes them to do so? That reason is given in the next two verses.

****

प्रकृतेः क्रियमाणानि गुणैः कर्माणि सर्वशः ।
अहङ्कारविमूढात्मा कर्ताहमिति मन्यते ॥ २७ ॥

Prakritehe kriyamaanaani gunaihi karmaani sarvashaha।
Ahamkaaravimudaatma kartaahamithi manyate॥

Actions are wrought in all cases by the *gunas* (modes) of nature. The egotistically deluded individual thinks that he is the doer. (27)

****

People do not understand that the cause of all action in the world is basically due to the modes of nature. The modes of nature means, the *gunas* of nature. Nature as such, is said to be constituted of the three *gunas*. Thus by the three modes of nature, all actions are being done everywhere, at all times.

What are the three modes of nature? Or what are the three constituent factors which go to make nature as such which is inert in character? This earth and the whole universe is nothing but an effect of this nature, or the modes of nature. Anything that is constituted of matter is nothing but an effect or an evolute of the three modes of nature. It is nature, *prakriti*, that is matter which has evolved itself into this panoramic universe. The mystics have perceived nature to be made of these three *gunas*, or characteristic qualities. Each is different in character. These three characteristics, *tamas*, *sattwa* and *rajas*, are symbolized by three colors. *Tamas* is symbolized by the color black, *sattwa* by the color white, and *rajas* by the color red.

These three modes, have characteristics of their own. *Tamas* leads to inertia and dullness, *rajas* is dynamic and always active, and *sattwa* has the quality of calmness, serenity, light, and brilliance. These three modes together in their various forms and combinations, have evolved into this physical universe.

In the beginning, the universe was in a subtle form, and thereafter got evolved into this gross universe. But prior to that the three modes of nature were equally balanced and were in a state of equilibrium. That state is said to be *prakriti* - nature, in an undisturbed, unmanifest condition. It is the potential seed state of the universe. Then what happens: that state of eveness of the three qualities gets disturbed. The dynamic aspect characterized by *the rajas* mode begins to be active and offsets the balance, and with that the entire creation begins to flow through. Thus thereafter anything found in the universe, possesses an aspect of each one of the three modes. There isn't anything in the universe which doesn't have any one of these three modes of nature. The universe is only an evolute of these three in various proportions.

Another word for *prakriti* is *maya*. The word *maya* is used for nature in its unmanifest condition. The universe is now manifest because the modes of nature have undergone a modification and as a result, have modified themselves into this physical universe. But prior to the universe being manifest, the universe was in an unmanifest potential condition. In that particular state the modes of nature were in a state of equilibrium or equipoise, undisturbed.

Then who brings about the disturbance? It is the Creator.

Nature by itself does not have the capacity. "Let me become this universe. Let me evolve myself into this universe." This is not possible for nature, for nature is inert. So there has to be a super-intelligent being, who is distinct from nature, and who brings about this disturbance in it. This Being is superior to the three modes of nature and unaffected by them. Thus the process of creation comes about and the whole universe evolves.

Everything in the universe is constituted of these three modes, including the human body. This physical body too, is an evolution of nature, of matter, an evolution of these three modes of nature. All the senses of knowing, viz. the organs of sight, hearing tasting, smelling, and touch which are the five organs of knowledge, *jnana indriyas*, are the evolutes of the modes of nature. Also the organs of action, the hands, the feet, the speech, etc. with which you do action in the world are the evolutes of the modes of nature. Thus the physical body, the ten organs, (the five organs of actions, and the five organs of knowledge), and the mind as well, are all evolutes of the modes of nature.

The mind too, is only subtle matter, and is also an evolute of the modes of nature. The mind thinks, and comes to a decision. All that is an activity of the mind. The mind is inert, but on account of it being an evolute of the luminous mode of nature (sattwa), it is luminous by nature. Thus the mind assumes a semblance of intelligence, and a semblance of consciousness. The Original Pure Divine Consciousness is reflected in the mind or percolates through it, and thereby the mind assumes intelligence and Consciousness with its reflected consciousness. Just as in a reflecting surface, reflection transpires, so also in the mind which is luminous in character, a reflection of the original pure consciousness transpires as it is made up of the *sattva* or luminous mode of nature. The *sattva* mode of the three *gunas*, is naturally luminous. As a result of it, you are able to discern things with the luminous mind. Therefore even though matter as such cannot discern, nevertheless with the luminous mind you can.

The mind, intellect, and the sense of ego are all modes of nature. Whatever functions in the universe is only a function of nature. So when your hand functions, and grasps something, it is only the mode of nature operating as the organ of action which grasps. Also, when you walk it is the legs which go about and take you from place to place. In this manner, all actions are only functions of the modes of nature. It is nature which functions. The tree grows. It is a very imperceptible motion. Your physical body also grows. You don't grow, it is only the body which grows, matures, and decays. Thus everything moves and changes in the whole universe. Wherever there is motion, it is a movement of nature in some form or the other. When the hands and the limbs move, it is also only a movement of nature in another form. Nature manifesting itself in a human form. It is nature which moves and creates motion. So also, when there is movement in the mind in the form of thoughts, which come and go. It is only a motion of the mind. The mind itself is only an evolute of the modes of nature. So Lord Krishna says any activity or motion is only brought about by the modes of nature. This is the cause of all action.

How does action proceed in the universe? What brings about action? It is a very natural thing for water to flow from a higher to a lower level. Also for the wind to blow. Every motion is a natural phenomenon of nature.

But just because you are in this physical body, you think that you are doing everything, and are the doer. When your eyes see, you think that you are the seer. The eyes cannot but see. That is the natural nature of the eyes to see. And when there is sound, naturally the ears cannot but hear. It is its natural nature.

The sound which is outside, which is to be heard by the ear, has come out of the same element of nature as the ear. Therefore, the ear has the capacity of hearing. The organ of hearing is able to hear, because it is produced out of the *akasa* element, the element of space. And sound is in space, correspondingly.

So also you are able to see with your eyes because the "sense of sight" has been produced out of the element called fire. And the element fire is the predominant factor in the vision world of forms. It is out of the fire element that the vision world has come about. Therefore, correspondingly, the eyes are able to see and not hear.

The tongue tastes food, because they are both evolutes of the same element water. And the nose is able to smell because the sense of smell, and the smell that is around you, have come out of the same earth element. Also the sense of touch, and air, have come out of the same element called air. Thus, the five-sense world has been produced and the corresponding sense organs have also been produced, and they do their natural functions.

Unfortunately, what has happened? The three modes of nature go on performing their various functions. When you are in a very calm state, and when you look, you have a gentle calm look, because you are calm and serene. When *sattva* mode is operative in you, then you are calm, serene and quiet. And when you look with your sense of sight, it is a gentle, pleasant look. But the three modes constantly keep on changing in your nature.

After a few hours or so, you may become angry. At that time, the *rajas* mode comes into your nature along with anger. At that time when you look, it is a hard look. The same eyes are looking, but now the character of looking has changed. It is a hard, angry look.

And soon after, you become a little lazy, when the *tamas* mode has set in and overpowered you. When *tamas* mode

139

overpowers you, you are in a lazy state, wherein you are not properly able to cognize things around you. You are now in a dull half-sleepy state. At that time, what type of a look do you have? An indistinguished look, wherein you are not able to properly discern things.

In all of these functions you will see that it is only the movement of the three modes of nature which has brought about the three different types of perceptions. Thus in all your activities and perceptions, it is the movement of the various modifications of nature. Even the body too, is a modification of nature. It is all nature which is in motion or movement. As per the three modes of nature, you keep on acting and reacting in the world.

Prakriteh gunaihi kriyamaanani karmaani. That is, the *gunas* (modes) of nature do all actions. This being the case, what happens is, your mind also modifies itself into a state of *ahamkara*, which means a state of egoism. Now your mind feels that "I am," and "I am so and so." Egoism is the self-assertive principle in man which makes a person feel that "I am so and so." When this self-assertive principle manifests then you automatically begin to feel that "I am so and so." This sense of egoism, is also a function and a modification of the mind. It is the mind which has now modified itself as the ego. The mind keeps on thinking both relevant and irrelevant thoughts all the time. When it mechanically keeps on thinking, then it is called the mind. When the very same mind undergoes the principle of self-assertion, then it is called the ego. When asked, "Who are you?" the man who has a bigger ego will not reply back directly and say who he is. He will instead say, "Don't you know who I am?" That's where the self-assertive principle comes in, or "I'll show you who I am." The person begins to feel that he is the self-assertive principle. He has identified himself with the self-assertive principle which is also a function of the mind. That self-assertive principle has identified with the mind, with the senses, and with the body. With this ego, the individual functions thinking that he is the doer and enjoyer.

Ahamkara vimudatma. The individual who has deluded himself with the ego notion, feels that he is the doer. This self-deluded individual has involved himself with this self-assertive ego principle called *ahamkara* and feels that *karta aham iti manyate* (I am the doer.) Thus this person has identified himself with the body, with the ten sense organs, and with the mind, and the intellect. He feels that he is this physical body, and begins to act as such. Whenever the body acts, he thinks he is acting. Whenever the senses act, he thinks he only acts. When the hands grasp, he thinks he is grasping, because his identification with the hands is so strong. When he is eating, he thinks that he is eating. But it is only the mouth which munches. When you put something into the mouth, automatically you begin to munch, and eat. But his identification is so intense, he feels that he is eating. All these feelings are so strongly ingrained in his ego character. As a result, he has the feeling that "I am the doer."

Actually the doership belongs to the body and the senses, which get activated by the mind. The doership belongs to all of these, but actually it is not even doership, it is just a movement of nature in this body with respect to the hands and the feet. It is the movement with respect to the body, the senses, and the mind. With all of these things, there is only the movement of the modes of nature. But being identified with it, he feels that he is the doer. So because of this, he is self-deluded in his own mind.

Ahamkara vimudaatma, that is, deluded with ego. He has been confused or confounded into thinking that he himself is the doer. He has this self-delusion that he is the doer. On account of this, he is attached to action and to the modes of nature functioning in his body. As a result of all this, there is this sense of attachment. This is how the ignorant man functions. But the wise man possesses this unique knowledge, about the way nature functions in the universe, and how he is distinct from nature itself. The person who doesn't have this knowledge or understanding, naturally feels that he is the doer, and begins to feel and act in that manner.

As he so considers, so he thinks. Opposed to this, we have the way by which a wise man who possesses this enlightened knowledge, acts in the world. Such a man knows well that he is not the doer at all. A man who has this knowledge understands how nature functions, and how he is distinct from nature. In the next verse we see.

****

तत्त्वविनु महाबाहो गुणकर्मविभागयोः ।
गुणा गुणेषु वर्तन्ते इति मत्वा न सज्जते ॥ २८ ॥

Tatvavittu mahaabaaho gunakarma vibhaagayoha|
Gunaa guneshu vartanta iti matva na sajjate||

O mighty-armed but the knower of truth, of the divisions of the modes (of nature) and their functional action knowing that *gunas* as senses move amidst *gunas* as objects, is not attached.   (28)
****

In contrast to the earlier person who was ignorant, this man is well-informed, and is a knowledgeable person who has a fine understanding of the truth of things.

What is this knowledge? That nature is nature and it is inert in character. That all functioning is done by nature. That in his essential nature, he is distinct from nature, even though a human. While the previous man was identified with his human nature in the form of the body, mind, intellect, and the senses. As a result of that identification, he feels that he has a human nature. Because of this identification with the body, with the intellect, and with the senses, the man develops this human nature, and feels that he is a human being. On the contrary, a man who has a good perspective and a good knowledge, knows the distinction. He knows that he is distinct from nature, which is inert, and which is in constant motion. Mobility is its nature and there is constant action. Incessant activity is the very rhythm of nature.

But he, as the *Atman*, is motionless, ever steady, and calm. There is no activity at all, and this *Atman* is self-luminous. Self-luminous means that it is not inert, and is self-aware of its own existence, which is ever steady and motionless. Such a man has the knowledge of *Atman* as *Atman* and nature as nature. Nature is inert, while the *Atman* is knowledge, wisdom, and awareness. On knowing the nature of the *Atman*, such a person is said to be a *tatwa vid*, who knows the truth of things.

There are only two things. One is the *Atman*, which is the Divine, and the other is the universe which is inert by nature. The knower of Truth has a complete and fine knowledge that they are two distinct things.

'Arjuna, you too are also capable of being a knower of the truth and are capable of being a *yogi*.' The word *mahabaaho* refers to Arjuna, and means "mighty armed or long armed." According to the characteristics of the body, a persons nature can be discovered. The type of body and the type of face reveal the character. The face is the index of the mind. By knowing the face and the way the body is structured, the person is known. Thus a person who has long arms, is capable of being a *yogi*. 'So Arjuna, it is not that you are not capable of this knowledge, it is very much within your capacity, and you can be a *yogi*.' So he is inspiring him by the word *mahabhaaho*, long-armed.

Not only is the *tattwa vid* a knower of the truth, of the *Atman* and inert nature, but is also a knower of how inert nature evolves

143

and functions. Once you understand nature, you will also understand how nature has evolved as the universe, and as this physical body. Therefore, he who has this understanding, the *tatvavid*, knows the truth of things, and thus knows the distinction between the *gunas* and *karma*. He knows the classification of the three *gunas*, and also knows the classification with respect to *karmas*. He knows how actions are brought about by the three *gunas*. Such a person, is not deluded. He knows that all actions are the movement of the *gunas* or the modes of nature.

As for the way the mode of your nature, so is your activity. If your mode of nature at the moment is *sattwa*, then you are calm and serene. Then naturally that serenity is manifest in all your actions and functions. On the other hand, when you have the *rajas* mode of nature operative in you, then naturally at that time, dynamism is manifest in your activities. You are restless, ever in incessant activity. When the *guna* is in the *sattwic* state, then you are quiet, and there is a temporary lull in the activity. When the mode of *tamas* takes over, then confusion and laziness prevail. Thus the modes of nature keep on alternating.

The knower of the truth of things knows that it is only the modes of nature which are in operation, on account of the fluctuations of these three *gunas*.

The person who has understood the classification and the division with respect to this, knows that it is the *gunas*, the modes of nature which has manifested and evolved as the sense organs. It is also these modes of nature, which have evolved as the sense objects too. The truth knower knows that the sense organs, are an evolute of the *gunas*, and that these sense organs naturally come in contact with their respective sense objects which in turn are also an evolute of the modes of nature. So it is the modes - *gunas*, which come in contact with the *gunas*, modes. *Thus gunaaha guneesu vartante -*

the modes of the sense organs come in contact with the modes of the sense objects. It is their natural function.

The organ of sight naturally comes in contact with the corresponding object, which is form. The sense-of-hearing naturally comes in contact with its corresponding counterpart, which is the sound world. The sense-of-taste comes in contact with its corresponding taste world. The sense-of-smell, comes in contact, naturally with the world of scent. If you go into an elevator, you cannot avoid smelling the perfumes, and want to get out of it as quickly as possible. Or you go into any place where there is a smell, and you instantly notice it. You cannot but smell. You cannot but taste. When you drink and eat something, the watery sense of that brings about a natural taste. Either it is sour, or tastes salty or sweet. As far as the tongue is concerned, it automatically tastes. When it is salty, it knows there is salt. The sense-of-taste immediately comes in contact with the object of the taste, and experiences it. It knows immediately. So also with all other senses, the sensation is there automatically. Therefore it is the senses which naturally go through their sensation with their respective counter-parts. *Gunaaha guneesu vartante.*

The enlightened person, *tattwavid*, knows this well. He knows that sensation is all due to the functioning of nature, and thereby is not attached. Not attached means that he does not feel that he is the doer, taster, or the person who is smelling, seeing, and hearing. He does not have the feeling that he is doing all these things. He knows the ears are hearing. Are you hearing? No, the ears are hearing. Of course, your mind is attached to the organ of hearing, therefore, the hearing is there. It gets registered, and you become conscious of it. So what is hearing? The ears are hearing. The eyes are seeing. Thus all these functions are done naturally by nature. But then, you get identified with each one of these senses, and

145

immediately begin to say, "I am hearing, I am seeing." The identification immediately comes to a normal man. But a wise man knows through discernment, that these acts are only the functioning of nature and no more than that.

Therefore, the feeling that I am the doer, the enjoyer, the eater, the drinker, and that I am the seer, is not there in the wise.

There is a nice episode about Lord Krishna with respect to this. One day, Krishna was on the bank of the river Yamuna. Some of the *gopis*, the women-admirers of Krishna came that way. Krishna said, 'It seems that the great sage Dhurvaasa has come here and you will do well to go and see him and get his blessing.' Accordingly, the following day the women got together and prepared various delicious foods to take to the great sage.

But it so happened, that morning, the river was swollen with high water. So the women could not cross the river to the other bank where the sage was. The boats too did not help. So the women *gopis* came and told Krishna, 'We have prepared all these delectable eats for the sage, will you help us cross the river?'

He told them, 'Well I will do it, but first why don't you ask Yamuna herself to allow you to cross the river? Just tell her that Krishna is a *brahmachari*, a celibate. On hearing it, the river Yamuna would allow you to cross the river. That is, make way for you.'

The *gopis* said amongst themselves, 'This Krishna is telling us that he is a celibate, but he has two wives and perhaps countless other *gopis* as well and has such a reputation, too. And now he is telling us that he is a celibate from infancy. This is too much for us to swallow. Anyhow, our purpose is to cross the river, never mind if he is or not, but let us cross the river. Anyhow we will tell Yamuna that this is what Krishna said, that he is a celibate and that you would give way for us to cross the river.'

This is just like Moses when he was leading the Jews out of exile from Egypt. At that time they had to cross the Red Sea. It is said, the Red Sea parted, and they were all able to cross. In the same way, Yamuna River parted its way, and allowed them to pass. But now they had to get back. So they appealed to the sage. So the sage told them, 'Tell Yamuna that Dhurvasa sage has not eaten anything, and the river will give way and you can cross to the other side.' The *gopis* were amazed at the words of the sage, for he had just eaten everything that they had brought. 'Krishna is pulling our leg. But to imagine the sage also doing so is too much. Anyhow now we are hungry and have to get back home. All we are concerned is to get back to the other side.'

Thus, the *gopis* uttered the sage's words, and to their amazement, the river Yamuna parted, and they were able to cross. Only if it is a true statement will the river part its ways. But it did. So now the *gopis* were even more baffled. To Krishna they said, 'We cannot understand this. We told Yamuna what you said and the river parted. For, whatever you say is true. Also the sage Dhurvasa says something and it is a statement of truth. If not the Yamuna would not have parted, and we wouldn't be here. We do not understand this!'

So Krishna explained to the *gopis*, 'The reason is, the sense of doership is not there. Dhurvasa *rishi* of course did not feel that he was the eater. It was the hands which were putting the food into the mouth, and the mouth was automatically swallowing it. So the sage knew that he was not the eater. If you have such an attitude then you are not the eater, nor the doer of anything.'

The sage in his wisdom knew that it was only the *gunas*, the modes of nature which is functioning. The modes of nature in the form of the hands is putting the food into another mode of nature, the mouth. Therefore, it is only a functioning of nature, and the sage has nothing to do with it.

If there is food, what happens if you are hungry? Automatically it enters the mouth. If the stomach is hungering for food, do you have to invite the man who is seated in front of the food, to take it? Automatically, without him knowing, the hands will move towards the food. If there is a form in front of you, you don't have to tell the person to look at the forms around him. The eyes will naturally be seeing. And when there is music being played, you don't have to tell the man to listen to the music. The ears are already listening. These are natural functions which are being done all the time. The idea is that the seer is detached from the seen and the acts of seeing.

The one who has this enlightened perspective or understanding, is detached from being identified or involved or becoming one with the various sense organs and their sensations. Therefore, he does not have this feeling that he is the doer. Such a person knows well, that it is nature which does everything. Since it is nature that is doing everything, as the eyes cannot but see, the ears cannot but hear, therefore there need not be any response one way or the other. The eyes are seeing, the ears are hearing, the senses are performing their natural functions. As a result of the senses performing their natural function, one has only to be a mere observer of the sense-activity. It is nothing but a detached perspective. It is a detached state of awareness because there is no response on your side, that I am the seer, that I am the eater, doer, etc.

Therefore, as a witness you are witnessing the movement of nature, the movement of the senses, the motion of the body, and everything else. So with the detached sense of perspective, you are observing and witnessing all that is going on around you. Like a witness consciousness, you are going about your deeds and activities. Your hands are going about doing what they have to do. Your legs are going about walking, and doing what they have to do. All these things are naturally being done with a detached perspective on your side. There is only mere awareness.

For a person who has this enlightened understanding, there is only a detached awareness of things. There is only an awareness which is aware of the functioning of nature. The body, too, is nature. Thus you are aware of the operations which are going on through it and around it. Therefore it is said, it is the *gunas*, the modes of nature, which function among the other modes of nature. Therefore, such a person does not do anything. Once this is understood, you too, in your own life, can now gradually attain to this state of detached awareness. With a detached sense of awareness, you just go about living and functioning in the world, in a calm, and serene manner.

You were previously involved in the world, through your senses and with the body. Now you have to get detached from all of them, and have your awareness detached too, as your consciousness was identified and involved with the functioning of nature. So now you have to recapture your true nature, as the actionless Atman. Thus gradually you are getting your awareness detached from its previous involvement. The functions of your body and senses are going on, but you are having a detached perceptive. With the detached perspective, like an observer, you are observing life around you. You are thus mindfully functioning, mindfully living, mindfully walking,

You are also observing the movement or the motion of the body and the senses. As a result, you are getting gradually disentangled. You were previously entangled with your senses and your body. Also through the senses, you got entangled with the sense-objects as well, and were truly identified and caught in it. Now you are getting disentangled in your awareness, with this detached perspective. Thereby you develop the capacity of choiceless awareness. Eventually, you will abide in this pure awareness and become totally Aware. This is how you get back to your true being, and for which purpose the science of action is being taught.

The Lord Krishna further says in the next verse:

****

प्रकृतेर्गुणसम्मूढाः सज्जन्ते गुणकर्मसु ।
तानकृत्स्नविदो मन्दान् कृत्स्नविन्न विचालयेत् ॥ २९ ॥

Prakriter gunasammuudaaha sajjante gunakarmasul
Taanakrtsnavidho mandaan kritsvavinna vicaalayathll

Those deluded in the modes of nature are attached to the modes and their actions.
The knower of truth should not upset (the minds) of those who are dull-witted and ignorant.   (29)

****

But ignorant people deluded by the functioning of the *gunas* of nature get attached to the *gunas* in their various forms of actions. The ignorant in the absence of this fine understanding, automatically get attached to the functioning of the *gunas*.

Having the ego as the basis, people are attached in this manner as they are identified with their body, senses, mind and the intellect. As a result, they get attached to the functioning of the body and the senses in their various functions and activities.

Therefore, he says, "*Taan akrithsnavidhomandaan krithsnavid na vichalayeet.*" The wise possessed of complete understanding should not unsettle the dull possessed of incomplete knowledge. *Mandaan* here means the person who has a dull mind, an unenlightened mind. A person can be highly intelligent, but in a spiritual sense, does not have this enlightened wisdom, and therefore is said to be wanting in knowledge and wisdom. He is thus referred to by the word dull. Spiritually dull in wisdom. *Akritsnavid* means

150

the ignorant person who does not have the total perspective. He lacks the complete vision of the Truth of life.

What is the perspective of the totality of life and existence? It is the Divine which is one and the totality of existence. Thus a person who has a total understanding of the Divine principle, and whose life is based on that principle, should not disturb the minds of the ignorant. For the ignorant are functioning with their dull mind. Such people's understanding should not be upset, or disturbed by the wise who have the understanding of the whole.

A person already engaged in action ignorantly is still attached to the actions, as he is involved with the modes of nature, and does not know it so. Therefore, he is attached to the actions of nature. If such a person is straight-away told that the *Atman* is actionlessness, may stop doing what he has been doing. His mind will be upset. Therefore, the wise should not upset that person, but rather, encourage him into action. Thereafter, counsel and tell him that there is a better way of doing actions, without a sense of identification. Thus the person will arrive at the understanding, and will not stop action, which will bring about his wane and destruction.

Spiritual advice has to be carefully given, as the people who come for it, listen to you, and live by it. Therefore when they listen their understanding gets cleared. The science of action will be enunciated in the next verse from another perspective.

Verses 30 - 34

Thus far, Lord Krishna was revealing the technique of *karma yoga*, whereby one converts action into a *yoga* of action. That is converting *karma* into *karma yoga*. That which brings it about is an enlightened understanding. And that knowledge towards it, was revealed by Lord Krishna. Initially when a new knowledge and an understanding gets first imparted, it does not easily get grounded in the mind of the hearer. Therefore, again and again, or in different ways, it has to be re-taught and re-reinforced.

For, *karma yoga* is the principal spiritual discipline for the man of the world leading an active life. It is his main spiritual discipline as he is daily beset with actions awaiting to be done. That which makes it so is an enlightened understanding. In *karma yoga*, it is not what you do which is important, but how you do, or with what attitude you do what you have to do. What you have to do happens to be your daily obligative functions. And these daily obligative functions are either your normal household duties, or your functions in the office, or your social obligations. All of these comprise the daily obligative functions which an individual undergoes every moment of his life.

He is now revealing the technique by which these functions which are the actions of *karma* could be converted into a *yoga*, which will liberate you in course of time. This *yoga* will release you from the bondage of action. Action when done ignorantly leads to bondage, because a person does actions being either involved with the fruits of actions, or the action itself. As a result, he creates a bondage complex therein. Thus he is revealing the technique by which, without being caught into those bondage complexes he would be in a position to convert action into an emancipating discipline. Into a *yoga* which leads him to liberation and enlightenment.

With respect to that, Lord Krishna is once again saying, in the thirtieth verse:

****

मयि सर्वाणि कर्माणि संन्यस्याध्यात्मचेतसा ।
निराशीर्निर्ममो भूत्वा युध्यस्व विगतज्वरः ॥ ३० ॥

Mayi sarvaani karmaani sannyasya adyatma chetasal
Nirashirnirmamo bhutva yudyasva vigatajuorahall

Having renounced all actions on me with spiritual discernment and being free of desire and without the sense of mine, may you engage in battle free of anxiety.   (30)

****

The word *sanyasya* means having renounced. But in this context, what he means is, not that he is asking you to renounce actions altogether but rather to dedicatedly perform those actions without a sense of ego. The "I" sense is to be renounced. He is enjoining you to perform action with the attitude of sacrifice dedicating it unto the Lord. Thus as a dedicated action the fruits of it are renounced. As you are performing actions with a sense of sacrifice, it is a sacrifice. Moreover you are renouncing the fruits of action too. Thus when you are performing actions as a sacrifice, it is a *yagna*. He had mentioned what an *yagna* is in the earlier verses too. Thus in this manner action becomes a renunciation. Vide verse nine.

Therefore he says, 'Having renounced the fruits of actions in this manner as a sacrifice unto Me, do what you have to do.' When he uses the words "unto Me," do not take it literally. When he uses these words he is identifying himself as the Creator who has taken a human form as Sri Krishna, the *avatar*, the messiah. From the point of view as the Creator, the Creator is the inner controller, and the Lord of this universe. Hence from that point of view he is referring to himself by the words, "unto Me." So "unto Me" as the inner controller and the overlord of the universe, may you dedicate all your actions.

For, whatever actions come your way in life, have already been ordained and schemed out for you by the Creator Himself. The Creator who has created this universe, has thereby also schemed out for each individual the volume of work to be done before departing from this life. With respect to your scheme of life, he has worked out your daily functions and duties which you are to perform like a boss daily assigning work to his employees. These daily functions and duties which you are to go through in life, have been worked out, keeping in consideration your prior life styles and development which you had undergone in your previous lives. Your prior development in your previous lives, has been considered along with your prior mental thoughts, feelings, and *karmas* that you had gone through. Keeping all these factors in mind, the Lord Himself has worked out for your own further good, and further evolution, a scheme of life in which the actions are to be done. It has been worked out for you, considering your impulses, mental and emotional development, as per your previous lives. He has schemed this out for you so that you can further develop yourself in this life. He has worked out these *karmas* to be unfolded in your life as years go by. Thus it is only proper for you to carry them out. Just execute, and work out what has already been ordained and worked out for you.

Thus it is only an ignorant man who feels that he is the doer. As the actions have already been worked out for you, just execute them as an instrument. In the process, if you feel that you are the doer, then you are merely assuming and atrogating responsibility and naturally will have to reap the fruits of it too. But on the other hand, if you had the good sense to know that all actions have been assigned to you, by the Big Boss, all that you would do is just execute them. By that you become a *nimitta*, an instrument. You become an instrument for actions.

In the Gita, Lord Krishna had revealed the final end of the war, even before the war took place in the Vishwarupa episode of the cosmic-form. In it he had revealed what the final outcome of the war was going to be. He had said, 'Don't imagine that you are doing this, it has already been done by me. You will only be an instrument for the action, and no more.' As an instrument, you merely execute whatever comes. Since the actions have already been schemed and worked out for each and everyone in the universe by the Lord, who is the Cosmic Architect, therefore it is only proper to do those actions which he has assigned for you. Why assume responsibility over it? Merely execute action because it has to be done either willingly or even unwillingly by you. With that your function is over.

Furthermore, he says, 'While you are doing action, fix your mind in Me. Perform actions with dedication and at the same time, fix your awareness in Me. Keeping Me in your mind, keep on performing actions. Thus you are not centered in the action, but are centered in Me.' *Adyatma chetasa* here means you are centered in the Divine, which is the reality, and true nature of your own *Atman*. *Atman* is your own true essential nature, and not your human nature. By maintaining your poise in your essential nature, you are centered in your true being. Thus by maintaining your awareness in your Divine nature, keep on performing these actions. Thus centered in the Divine, keep on doing all that you have to do and which has to be done by you in the world. Thereby you merely go through the operations of action and living.

Normally a person's mind is either centered in himself or in the things of the world, but here he is now centered in his Divine nature. Therefore, very effortlessly, and peacefully, without any anxiety, he goes through his functions in a detached manner.

Then with what attitude should we go about doing these functions? The word *nirashi* means without desire. When a person gets into an action with the desire for the results of those actions, then those very desires along with the hope for it, bring about anxiety. Thus when you become anxious over what you are doing, naturally you will not be able to perform these actions well and peacefully. The action will be done now with tension and uncertainty. Therefore he says, "*vigata juoraha.*" Be free of anxious sorrow, by becoming free of desire for its results.

For the results of all action automatically accrue according to their own laws. Thus you don't have to be anxious about them. For whatever you have done, the result is bound to follow. You have no control over the outcome. The only control you have is over what you are doing at the immediate present. The purpose of life is to live the present, to be busily involved with the present. So when you are busily involved with the present, which is the immediate matter at hand, which is life, then living itself gets taken care of. When you take care of your present, the future automatically gets taken care of. When the present functions and actions are very calmly and effortlessly taken care of, then it gets well done. When a thing is well done, the anxiety over its outcome ceases.

When the present action is well-taken-care-of, its outcome too will be the best as it could be. Whatever it be, be prepared to accept the outcome one way or the other. It does not matter. For the balanced living of life is more important than the little success and failure that you encounter. When you are able to maintain your activity of life without this anxiety and expectation, then naturally you will go through your duties in a very peaceful way, with a peaceful mind. One of the definitions for *yoga* is *samatwam yoga uchate*. *Yoga* is the state of mental equipoise. Yoga is a science of mind. If you are going to live life, going through your actions in a very calm and peaceful manner, without being ruffled, then that is said to be the state of *yoga*, the desired state. This particular state will lead you to the ultimate state of total peace. Thus, don't ever imagine that if you do not learn to live in peace now, that you will attain total peace later. Therefore this state of mental equipoise has to be very carefully looked into and maintained by a *karma yogi*.

Arjuna was saying, 'I shall be killing these people, and they are my people.' Thus he had the feeling of mineness. Hence without feeling that these are my people and my things, go ahead and do what you have to do, as duty. Don't allow your personal feelings and considerations to come and blind you in matters of duty. When you have these feelings you are unable to do what is right and get into a field of action. For, when you have the feeling of mineness, that is delusion, *moha*. Delusion or *moha* overpowers your character and nature. Thereby you are unable to see what is right and proper. The ability to discriminate and see things in their true light is lost. Hence do what you have to do, duty bound, without this feeling that these are my people, and my teachers and kinsmen with whom I have to engage in battle, and perhaps kill.

Just like a judge, who with all impunity, was sentencing everyone in the court of law, who had done crimes. But when his own son was called into the court for a particular offense, he began to get misplaced emotions. He thought, for after all, this youngster is a little boy of 18 years. Perhaps he may have not done knowingly. So these considerations come into the mind of the judge, and he is unable to sentence his own son because of the feeling that he is "my son." Prior to that he was able to dispense justice without any difficulty. So is the case here with Arjuna too.

This is one of the problems in life. In the world, people are unable to take a just position because of this personal factor or mineness that comes in and interferes in good judgment in matters in life. Hence, Krishna says, 'Without having this feeling that they are my people, go ahead and get into this inevitable action of war which has come to you.' Krishna tells Arjuna to get into this war, which happens to be his duty.

Vigatajuora means free of heat, or a sense of disquiet. That sense of disquiet brings about uncertainty. And uncertainty leads to lack of action, and non-performance of duty. Hence boldly and vigorously get into this action without the feeling of mineness and without the heat of anxiety over its outcome.

****

ये मे मतमिदं नित्यमनुतिष्ठन्ति मानवाः ।
श्रद्धावन्तोऽनसूयन्तो मुच्यन्ते तेऽपि कर्मभिः ॥ ३१ ॥

Ye me matamitham nityamanutishtanti maanavaaha।
Sraddhaavanto anusuyanto muchyante teapi karmabhihi॥

Those people who always practice this teaching of mine with faith and without sarcasm, get liberated from actions. (31)
****

This particular doctrine which I have just revealed, is a way of living. Those people who follow this teaching, practice and live by it, imbued with faith, get released from action. Faith according to religious literature means faith in the words of the scripture and faith in God.

There is no such thing called blind faith in the world. Faith always comes through understanding, and appreciation. When you say, "I have faith in my employee," it means having understood the employee, you have faith in him. When a man says, "I have faith in my wife," having known his wife, he has faith in her. When the wife says, "I have faith in my husband," knowing who her husband is, she has faith in him. When the children say, "I have faith in my father," knowing the father, they have the confidence called faith.

There is no such thing called blind faith, as it is an expression freely used in the world. You will always find that faith is something which grows in a person through experience. As a person keeps on living in the world, subconsciously and unconsciously he keeps on developing faith in matters of life. As a person keeps on living life, and goes through the scriptures, and listens to the words and instruction of the wise, develops faith in time.

By living in the world, you begin to realize that there must be a super-intelligent principle though you have not seen it. You have not experienced God, but nevertheless, people do have a faith that there is a God. What makes them have this faith? As they keep on living and experiencing life, and seeing the way things are happening around them, and the way many things happen in their own life too, then this faith that there must be a higher intelligence which is guiding this universe and guiding their life too, naturally grows.

Faith also implies faith in the words of the scriptures, and in the good words of the teacher. As you keep on meeting the teacher, and having a dialogue with him, then you begin to develop a faith in his wisdom and understanding, and also develop a faith in him too. This is called *sraddha*, faith. And when you begin to have this faith, then you begin to listen to the words, and live by it.

Why is it that little children listen implicitly when they are very small, and later on begin to question? Implicitly, they listen to the words of the parents because they have faith in them. When you tell little children something, they listen to you. But later on when they find out what you tell them is not quite correct, then they begin to lose faith in you. Initially they have that faith but later on, when you begin to tell lies, and say wrong things, the child begins to realize it. Then he begins to lose faith and questions. Not till then. Till then his faith carries him through early life.

Here also you begin to have faith in the master, in his words and wisdom. Faith also in the words or the teachings of the scriptures too. You begin to realize that the scriptures are giving you a unique knowledge and understanding. It is not only giving you that knowledge, but is also supplying you with a certain measure of reasoning too. A reasoning which enables you to gradually develop or acquire faith. Hence Krishna says, 'Those people who have listened to this teaching of mine, understood it, and having understood, live by it imbued with faith shall be emancipated from life and its actions.' This is what the scripture declares as the Truth because there is no other way for you to know. You have to get your learning somewhere. The learning in the world will give you worldly knowledge. But here is a super-mundane knowledge, a learning which is teaching you about your super-mundane transcendental existence.

There are only three sources of information which reveal to you how to attain this extraordinary state of enlightenment. One source is wherein the Creator himself takes a human birth, becomes a messiah, and gives you the message or the teaching, and performs miracles to induce faith in him and his words. Then the scriptures too are a revelation. In that too, you begin to develop a faith. And thirdly, in the words of the wise. You will find that the enlightened people, the great sages and seers seem to have a measure of wisdom, which a normal person does not possess. They have a measure of knowledge, which is not available to a normal person. Thus faith is a compound of higher emotion, reverence and humility towards something which is benign, good and wholesome.

Thus you have to expose and open your mind to a new type of knowledge which you are not aware of. You are a pilgrim living in this world, and life is a pilgrimage. When you are living in this world as a pilgrim, you do not know your bearings in life. Of course you know your worldly bearings, but apart from that, you are not very sure and clear about the spiritual bearings of life. In order to get your directions as to how to live a spiritual life, you may have to take refuge in the words of the enlightened, and in the masters, and the scriptures. By and by, the faith in leading a new life develops in due course.

Sraddhaanto anasuyanto means those people who are imbued with faith, and who do not cavil and are not sarcastic towards the master and his teachings and do not cast words of aspersion at the teacher. Those people who do not have this character will receive the blessings of the gods and the holy men. Once you have obtained the words of wisdom from a holy being, and realize his nobility and greatness, then thereafter, you do not begin to cavil at him.

There are certain people who only see a black spot anywhere. They keep on looking for it and thereby blacken everything. It is all due to their impure and warped mind. If it does not come up to their own personal standards of pride, prejudice, ignorance, and arrogance, then they immediately blacklist the whole person. On the other hand there are certain other people who look into the good and positive aspect overlooking the innocuous and harmless human frailties of life.

But here, the seeker knows the master, Krishna very well. Lord Krishna is known very well as the messiah, as the incarnate teacher giving here in the Bhagavad Gita the message and the teaching to the human race.

The world has been awaiting such a savior all the time. The savior too comes, gives a saving teaching and then departs. It is the duty of the human race too seek out this teaching, live and mold their life accordingly and get liberated.

The savior comes to give a liberating teaching. It is the living and the practice of the good teachings which will save a man from the bonded life on Earth and take him to a heavenly state of well-being beyond the realm of encased life in matter. In it the spirit of the soul is ever free to abide in its pristine pure blissful state of being, unfettered by matter with its accompanying travails of effort and the struggle to live. Therefore such a wondrous state of struggle-free existence is heavenly, desired by one and all, and attained at enlightenment. Enlightened to the full bloom of Godly being. This is the be-all and end-all of life.

He says, 'Those that do not cavil at Me, who do not mock and insult Me, having understood Me as the Creator who has taken this human form, get liberated in course of time.' These are words that he is uttering, they are words coming out of a great being. For, it is seen in the world that people mock at holy beings and their good teaching.

There was a man who was coming here for the soul-elevating classes, and he told a few others that he would be unable to attend a certain party on account of having to attend the religious discourses. One amongst them said, "*swamijiko bhagat bangaya*," that is, "Have you become a devotee of the *swami*?" Thus they are indirectly mocking the person. When a person wants to go and do something which is good, they laugh and mock at him. But those people with good feelings who look upon the teacher and his words get liberated from life and life's actions in the world.

How do these people get liberated? By going through their actions as *karma yoga*. This brings about the purification of the mind. Once the mind is purified, the subsequent discipline called *jnana nista*, the state of being totally absorbed in meditation, automatically transpires. In meditation one is totally absorbed in the Divine. Thereafter, one gets enlightened. When that takes place, you get liberated from all actions, from life, and from this universe, and attain to the pristine pure state.

****

ये त्वेतदभ्यसूयन्तो नानुतिष्ठन्ति मे मतम् ।
सर्वज्ञानविमूढांस्तान् विद्धि नष्टानचेतसः ॥ ३२ ॥

Ye tvatadabyasuuyanto naanutistanti me matam।
Sarvajnaana vimuutaanms taanviddhi nastaanachetasaha॥

Those people who cavail at my doctrine and do not follow it, being deluded of good knowledge, perish without spiritual discernment. (32)

****

In the next verse (32) Lord Krishna says, 'There are certain other people who *abyasuyanto*, cavil, not only Me, but mock at my teachings too.' Those people say, 'After all, what is there for us to get into this teaching, we have other things to do. There are better things to do in life. There are other systems of thought. Let us confine ourselves to our own way of thinking. Why unnecessarily bother ourselves with this teaching? For with this teaching, we have to assume a certain measure of responsibility and lead a responsible life. Why get into all this discipline? Let us keep on living the way we are living, which is easy and natural to us. Why unnecessarily get into this spiritual discipline of the living of life and temper our lives and our minds, and emotions? All of this requires effort. After all, it is so nice to live by way of the instincts and our thought patterns with which we have come into this world. Also according to the ideas which are prevalent in society let us live. It is an effortless and natural way of living. Why don't we keep on living like this, instead of getting ourselves involved in these teachings, by which we are to discipline ourselves, our minds, and our thoughts. It is a nuisance. This is a better way out.'

So there are certain people who think like this, and they dismiss the whole thing. 'It is not for us at the moment, we are busy with other things. Those people who have nothing else to do, can listen to the words of Krishna, and live by his teaching, but it is not meant for us.'

Thus Krishna says, 'There are certain people who talk or think like this, and do not follow my teaching. Neither do they understand, nor care to understand. They think they have a superior mind, and a superior intellect. After all, we are pretty smart people living in the world. It is meant for others. We are too smart for religious knowledge.'

There are people who think that way in the world. They do not even care to listen to the teachings and thus even care to live a noble life. What happens to these people? *Sarva jnana vimudaan*, being deluded of all knowledge, or being deluded to the all-knowing knowledge. These people get deluded, and confused in not having that all-comprehensive all-knowing knowledge. That is why it is said in one of the Upanishads, "What is that knowledge by which, all that which has to be known gets known?" Then that knowledge was revealed. That knowledge is said to be *Brahma vidya*, the knowledge of the Divine Reality.

Why is it considered to be the all-knowing knowledge? By knowing it, there is nothing left which is unknown in the world. By knowing it, all that has to be known is rendered known. That is the Divine, which inhers and exists in all things in the universe as its warp and woof. The Divine in the Hindu scriptures is referred to by the word *Brahman*. It is the only principle which exists and therefore by knowing it, all that which has to be known is know. That is the all-consuming totality of knowledge, for which the wholistic vision, the vision of the whole is necessary.

At the present moment in the day to day world around us, we have fragmentary and fragmented knowledge. The knowledge that is available has been fragmented into specialized knowledge. It is the knowledge of chemistry of the atoms, and chemical elements. Or it is a knowledge of physics, zoology, botany, mathematics, and so on. All different branches of knowledge. Each person becomes a specialist in a particular field. He may have good knowledge with respect to that field, and very little knowledge with respect to everything else, or a minimum knowledge with everything else, Even in his own field of knowledge, the knowledge is incomplete because all knowledge and sciences are developing. What you know today gets supplanted tomorrow or the next decade. There is a growth in the understanding of the sciences. Thus even in one science there is incompleteness.

But with the all-consuming knowledge, you find it is a knowledge which deals with the totality from a total perspective. The entire jig-saw puzzle of the universe and the mystery and the cause of the universe is understood in one stroke in a complete sense. Having known that, one Reality and thereby having obtained that knowledge, all individual knowledges automatically become available. If the need arises, those individual knowledges or sciences can also be known if a person wants.

These great mystics were said to be all-knowing. They knew all things which have to be known. If they wished to know, they could know. But they cared not to know, which is a different matter altogether. Nevertheless they had a knowledge which enabled them to know everything. The science of *Ayurveda* was not developed by experiment, but was mystically perceived. *Ayurveda* is herbal treatment of diseases. What herbs are meant for what disease. That is the science of *Ayurveda*. In South India it is also called *siddha vaidya*. Thereby meaning the practice of mystically known medicine.

Such super mundane knowledge is possible with this all-comprehensive knowledge of the one Reality, viz. the Divine.

Thus people are deluded by not knowing that all-knowing principle. By knowing that all-knowing principle, all is known. And these ignorant people, not knowing this, live in the world, without obtaining the proper understanding. Thus without knowledge, these people perish. They perish in the world in the sense that they keep on living in the world taking life after lifes. They keep on being born over and over again.

'If that is the case, what makes people not follow your teaching? What is that factor which prevents people from even caring to listen to your teaching? They are not interested even to listen to it, much less live by it. After all, you are the incarnate who has given the instruction. Don't these people have fear and reverence for God the Creator? But they go about living the way they want to live. Quite a good many people in the world live by their base instincts. They feel that we have the right to live any way we want to live. It is a personal right of ours, and we do not want to follow any particular discipline or way of living. We want to live by instincts. It is a free world, a free life, it is freedom to live. Thus why is it that these people are not afraid? Or do not even want to listen to your teaching?'

He replied, 'The reason is, everybody in the whole universe follows and lives by his own nature.'

****

सदृशं चेष्टते स्वस्याः प्रकृतेर्ज्ञानवानपि ।
प्रकृतिं यान्ति भूतानि निग्रहः किं करिष्यति ॥ ३३ ॥

Sadrisham chestate svasyaaha prakriterjnanavanapi।
Prakritim yaanti bhuutani nigrahaha kim karisyati॥

Even the wise act according to their own nature.
All beings follow their nature. What will restraint do?   (33)

****

Everyone in the world, inclusive of a wise man, lives as per his own nature, the character of his being. The nature of a man reveals his character. The nature of a person is made up of the impressions that he has. These impressions are said to be the *samscaraas* and the *vaasanaas*. The *vaasanaa* is a deep-rooted urge within man. *Samscara* (impressions) goes back to your previous lives. In those lives you had developed many thought patterns and had lived various life styles, and had various life-experiences. The impressions of those life-styles and life-experiences have been acquired by you. It is in fact you, and has become your nature. Whenever we experience something, or whenever we do something, automatically its impression is etched in the subconscious of the mind in the form of memories. Whatever actions, thought patterns, feelings emotions, learning patterns, desires, anger patterns, hatreds and passions have been developed ... all go to make the impressions in your mind. The sum total of all this is your samscaras.

And once the impressions become deep-rooted and you repeat them over and over again, it becomes a habit. Thus you develop strong inner urges, which are said to be your *vaasanaas*, the strong impulse within you. These urges and impulses are the operative force within. They lie dormant in the sub-conscious of your mind, and surface and manifest as per occasion. Thus the cause of those deep-rooted urges is within yourself. You have acquired and developed them in your previous lives and these urges and impulses are the characteristics that you have. The tendency to do good, to be mischievous, to be wicked, or to be saintly are all natural characteristics and tendencies which you have developed and acquired in lives before.

The cumulative factor of all this put together is said to be your immediate nature - *prakrirti*. It is that which is manifesting now, as your nature of being. Whatever talents you have is a talent which was acquired, developed, and cultivated by you in your previous lives and in this life it comes naturally to you as a talent: a talent for music, for art, or a talent in any particular field is an expression of your nature. Thus according to his nature every person is impelled and acts in the world. Even a wise man too, naturally acts as per his own nature. As per his own saintly nature, he tends to become a saint.

There are many types of enlightened people. Some of them have a dialogue with the world. In what manner would they have a dialogue with the world and live in it? They would live in the world, or have a dialogue with the world as per their prior impulses and habits. As per the way they had lived before and as per the tendencies which they had before. After enlightenment, too, they would naturally keep on living in that manner. There is nothing unusual or unique about it. Thus even a wise man lives according to his prior nature. If he has a habit to drink a particular beverage he would naturally only drink that. If he has a tendency to go for walks, he would naturally go for walks because it is a tendency which he has gone through before getting enlightened. If he has a tendency to wear particular types of clothes, he would keep on wearing the same clothes. If he was talking in a certain manner previously, in the same manner he would keep on talking subsequently. Thus these people behave here as per their own nature.

I came across a very interesting mystic. There were two very unique things about him: he never took food, and he never slept. He was brought to the United States and lived there until the age of about 110 or 112, and recently passed away. This particular sage had a peculiar habit, and that was to smoke cigarettes. He neither slept nor ate, and he was the kindest soul that I had met in my life. I had the good fortune to meet him about 35 years ago. This person must have developed this particular habit before he had become a wise person. Thus this habit was continuing thereafter. *Svasyaha prakriter sadrisham chestate jnanavan api.* Hence you find even the wise have lived and behaved according to their own previous nature.

In fact all creatures in the universe act according to their nature. The dog cannot but bark. If a dog does not bark, you wonder if it is a dog. You are satisfied if it barks even at you. Every creature in the whole universe naturally acts and behaves as per its natural tendency or nature which is said to be its *prakriti*.

This *prakriti* is the nature of a person. How did you acquire your nature? As per your previous lives. By the life styles that you had gone through and the actions that you had done, you had acquired good and bad impressions. Coupled with the good and the bad impressions of your previous lives, you had developed thoughts and desire patterns, too. Then along with the desire patterns, you had developed feelings, and other tendencies too. You had also cultivated particular talents. All these factors together become manifest as your own nature. Whatever you are now, did not come from nowhere, but is something which you yourself developed in your own being.

Therefore, a saint cannot but be saintly in nature, because that is his own nature. That is his natural character. There is no other way he can behave. That is the only way he knows how to behave. So also with every person. A cruel person knows only one way to behave, and that is to be very harsh and cruel. Because that is the way that he had trained himself to be, and that is now naturally manifesting itself. Each person cannot but be what he is. You cannot praise a saint for having been a saint because he couldn't help being what he is. So also, you cannot blame or condemn a man for being whatever he is, because he is what he is.

Therefore, *prakrithim yanti bhutani*. All beings and creatures act and move according to their nature. Not only that, in their nature, they are impelled by two powerful currents. The two currents in operation are *raga* and *dwesha* - likes and dislikes. Acute likes and acute dislikes. Impelled by likes, one keeps on getting into activities that one likes. When you have a strong liking for something, then impelled by that powerful motive force of attraction within, called *raga*, he courts objects, events, experiences, and people towards which he has a liking. Also impelled by dislikes, called *dwesha*, he tends to get away and recoil from objects, events, people and experiences from which he has a dislike. Motivated by these two powerful currents operating within, man operates his life. He courts things on one side, and recoils from the other. Thus you will find a man's daily activity is governed by these two powerful urges or motive forces within.

Prakritim yanti bhutani nigraha kim karisyati. Creatures tend towards their nature. Who can stop or restrain that? Neither I nor anyone else can prevent that. It is a natural process. A car which is in motion has to go through its motion, as it has acquired a momentum. Impelled by that momentum, it proceeds on. Thus impelled by his own nature, each person is what he is and does what he does and who can put a stop to it or prevent it? If that is the case, isn't there hope for man? If every person is a victim and is victimized by his own *prakriti* or nature, then cannot man have any hope for emancipation? Cannot a man hope for any change and hope for any modification in his nature? To this Krishna says:

****

इन्द्रियाणीन्द्रियस्यार्थे रागद्वेषौ व्यवस्थितौ ।
तयोर्न वशमागच्छेत्तौ ह्यस्य परिपन्थिनौ ॥३४॥

Indriyasyendriyasarthe ragatdweshou vyavastitou\
Tayor na vasamagachhat thou hiyasya paripanthinou\|

Attraction and aversion are naturally present in the senses towards their sense-objects. One should not come under their sway. They are your enemies. (34)

****

For, every sense organ comes in contact with its corresponding sense object. The sense of sight, has its corresponding object, the outside form world. It cannot but come in contact with it. The sense of hearing naturally comes in contact with its corresponding object, which is the sound world. Thus, every one of the sense organs, comes in contact with its corresponding sense object. The organ of taste comes in contact with its own taste world. When you eat food, the taste buds naturally taste food. The organ of smell, the olfactory organ, naturally comes in contact with its own smell world. So through the five senses, the form world, the sound world, the taste world, the sense world, and the touch world, are sensed. Thus is the universe sensed.

When they so come in contact, two factors are always present; *raga* and *dwesha*. There are natural likes and natural dislikes in such a process. The moment the sense of sight comes in contact with the form world, whatever it finds pleasant and conducive, is attracted to, and whatever it finds repulsive and unpleasant, it recoils from. It is so too for the sense of hearing. When it hears a jarring noise like the tooting of a horn, it recoils because it dislikes it, *dwesha*, and when pleasant music is being played, it immediately pricks its ear and listens because it is attractive.

Attraction and aversion are the twin currents of existence. These two sensations or experiences are inherently present in every sense contact of the senses, with their respective sense world. This is a natural phenomena. That being the case, you have a sensation every time either one of these forces come into play Either there is *raga* or likes and pleasantness and happiness; or there is unpleasantness, dislike, and sorrow. These two factors of *raga* and *dwesha*, likes and dislikes, are inherently present in every sensation and perception.

With respect to these he says, "*Tayor na vasamagacheth.*" Do not come under their sway. Do not fall a victim to their invasion. Why? *Thou hiyasya paripantinou.* They are your enemies. You are a pilgrim traveling in this world. As a pilgrim they rob you of your poise and waylay you into the sense world away from your path, and intended way of spiritual living. Like a thief, they distract you, and take your attention away. These two factors take your attention into the world, away from the purpose of life, which is to go beyond the sense world into the ineffable state of well-being.

If that be the case, in what manner should we not become a victim and not fall a prey to them? There is a way by which you would not be victimized by them, but be able to overcome them. That way is to follow and live by the teachings and the instructions which have been given to you thus far. Lord Krishna says, 'He who follows my teaching would be redeemed.' So when you are able to live by the teachings which you have obtained, with understanding and faith, then the living of life based on the teachings, would be the basis to function in the world.

The basis of living in the world is based on the wisdom teachings, and not based on your likes and dislikes. Therefore, whether you like or dislike something is irrelevant. But what is relevant is, you are going to live, condition, and temper yourself with the wisdom-teachings which are going to be the basis of your existence.

You are not going to base your human existence governed by likes and dislikes, which are the outcome of your instincts. You are not going to live by your instincts, which bring about likes and dislikes, but are going to base your existence, and the living of life, and go through your functions in the world based on enlightened understanding. Irrespective of whether you have likes or dislikes, you are going to do what has to be done because you are duty-bound to do it. Also whether you have likes or not, you are not going to do something which you should not do. The criterion for your doing and not doing something is based on the instructions of the available knowledge you have. It is not based on your personal likes and dislikes.

What normally happens is, because of likes, you would like to do something else, instead of doing what you have to do. Similarly, because of your dislikes, you do not feel like doing what you have to do. See the difference. But, what you have to do is, do your obligative duty and function. Because of your likes elsewhere, you do not want to do, and because of your dislikes you do not feel like doing it. Are your likes and dislikes going to be the governing factor of what you should do and what you should not do? Certainly not!

Therefore, the way to overcome your likes and dislikes, the way to overcome *raga* and *dwesha*, is to submit yourself to what you should do. When you submit yourself to the higher law of living and understanding, then based on it you are going to do what has to be done, irrespective of likes and dislikes. Thus, in this manner you gradually overcome your likes and dislikes. You do not anymore fall a prey and become a victim of them. It is in this manner that one does not come under the sway of likes and dislikes and thus overcomes *prakriti* or one's nature.

So the second line of the stanza has two factors. The first is, "One should not come under the sway of likes and dislikes." The second factor is, "In what manner should one not come under its sway?" By submitting oneself to the higher law of what should be done with an enlightened wisdom. When you follow this, then one does not come under the sway of likes and dislikes.

When you do not come under the sway of likes and dislikes, you are developing the capacity within yourself to modify and change your own nature. Otherwise, you get carried away, impelled by your nature, and remain the same good old person that you were before. But when you submit to the higher law, then you thereby tend to modify your nature. Thus there is hope indeed. This is the practical way by which you can bring about the change in your own nature and character.

Verses 35 - 38

It was mentioned by Lord Krishna that one should not yield to the forces of *raga* and *dwesha*, that is likes and dislikes which operate and victimize one. Instead, one should submit to the higher law of *dharma*, which governs the living of life. We have thus far been following this instruction. If we submit our lives, and temper our understanding, with enlightened wisdom, then thereafter one would acquire the capacity not to submit to the two forces of *raga* and *dwesha*, or likes and dislikes, which naturally operate in an individual. Thereby one rises above the two principal governing forces in a human being. By submitting to the higher law, one rises above these two impulses, which operate in a person, and thereby in course of time, overcome one's own *prakriti*, or nature. Gradually one acquires the capacity to rise above one's natural instinctive impulses. Therefore, one should submit oneself to the higher law which is the *dharma* of life.

In the next verse, he is going to tell you about *dharma*. When a person lives his life according to his own *dharma*, then that does him good. He says in the 35th verse:

****

श्रेयान्स्वधर्मो विगुणः परधर्मात्स्वनुष्ठितात् ।
स्वधर्मे निधनं श्रेयः परधर्मो भयावहः ॥ ३५ ॥

Sreyaan svadharmo vigunaha paradharmaath svanustitaath|
Svadharme nidhanam sreyaha paradharmo bhayavahaha||

One's own *dharma* of lesser merit is better than another's *dharma* even though well performed.
Death is better in one's *dharma*; another's *dharma* is fraught with fear.   (35)

****

One's own *dharma*, the law of living life, even though it be of lesser merit, is *sreyan*, better or superior to another's *dharma*, which is foreign to one's nature, even though it be well performed. One's own *dharma* is better for one's well-being than a *dharma* lived which is foreign to one's nature.

What exactly is *dharma*? There are various ways of defining the concept of *dharma*. You may call it righteousness, virtuous living, or righteous living in the English language. Or you may call it more appropriately, the law of being. The law of being of every person, is said to be his *dharma*. And this is unique to each being.

This word *dharma* unfortunately defies an appropriate English translation. Therefore, humorously it is said in India, of what use is it to study English, which has no *punya* or no *dharma* in its language. It is humorously said because the word *dharma* defies an appropriate English translation. You may call it righteousness, or the law of living, or virtuous life. But none of these words appropriately reveal the intrinsic implication of what this particular word denotes and conveys. We could say it is the law of being, for each being.

That law of being incorporates many factors. It is the law by which you are to live and conduct life. This law is based on universal cosmic laws which have been set in motion by the Creator for the well-being of the human race. That is one factor. The social laws of being which have been enacted by society are the second factor. Thirdly, it involves your own personal nature which is part of this "law of being." In fact it very much involves your personal nature which determines your way of life and law of being. This is a very important contributive factor, which goes to define and frame your *dharma* and law of being.

The universal cosmic laws are irrevocable and are valid for all times, in all countries, and for all people irrespective of race or creed. Examples are the law of *karma*, the law of gravitation and the law by which nature functions. All these come under the universal law of occurrence. It is not that there is a separate law of *karma* for an Indian, another for an American or Russian. These are universal laws which are in operation for all beings.

Then we have social laws which are very unique and which vary from country to country. These are the social norms, conventions, and practices. What is considered to be virtuous and proper in one country, may not be the same in another country. Even in one country, that which is considered as an appropriate social convention two thousand years ago, is no longer applicable today. For in time they change. These are the flexible laws governing human society at different places at different times.

The law of being, the law of existing, is said to be your *dharma*, or the way of living. Another way of saying is: it is the appropriate way by which you are to live and conduct your life. That appropriate way of living life known as *dharma* would promote your well-being and betterment. Such a concept, cannot be easily phrased, or translated into a particular word. It requires a paragraph, maybe a chapter to elicit it. Whatsmore, this law of being of oneself is governed by your intrinsic nature. The type of person that you are and your character make-up is a very important factor to determine your law of being. The norm by which you are to live and conduct yourself in life, in the society, and in God's creation. It is very much determined by your own personal character and propensities inherent within you. This will determine your law of being.

Therefore, Lord Krishna says, one's own *dharma*, one's own law of being, which is appropriate to oneself, is better than another's law of being, meant for another type and character. This is so even if one's own *dharma* is devoid of total merit, and contains faults and errors. You may be able to outwardly follow another's law of being, but cannot inwardly live it with your heart, because your nature would find it alien. It is not suitable for you. You may not be a king and be kingly, but you can play the part of a king. And sometimes even very well, too. But playing the part is only playing the part, and is not natural to your own nature. Because that is a character which is alien to you. You have to live and conduct yourself in a manner which is in accordance with and consistent to your own intrinsic nature.

Similarly too, one can be attracted to be a monk, and live the life of a hermit. But unless one has the qualities and the virtues to be so, one's life would be an error and whatsmore, one would not have the capacity to derive benefit from it. Thus such a life for one incompetent would be devoid of merit, as one would now be a sanctimonious being putting up a show of piety. That is hypocritically pious, as such a way of life is alien to one's nature, and therefore is not one's *dharma*.

For, to aspire to be a hermit-monk, one must first of all be holy and saintly in nature. For this one must be gentle, be kind, calm and compassionate, devoid of anger, arrogance, ill-will and hatred. One must be a noble soul with an inwardly drawn contemplative mind. Then with the presence of these virtues, one would be able to live a peaceful, serene and contemplative life of a monk, with love and good-will towards one and all.

Such a monk lives a life of piety, and simplicity, devoid of pride and arrogance and shuns ostentation, power, and display. He is a natural simple being, god and Truth-focused.

Until these qualities dawn in one, one should never be a monk. As being a monk or a nun is not a profession belonging to an ecclesiastical order. But is an inward call of the Spirit longing for God and Truth with all one's heart and being. Thus such a one is incapable of social work or service, and is incapable of servicing any institution. But lives a quiet life totally dedicated to prayers and meditation. It is a "prayerful life," reverently lived, and only such a life sanctifies and leads one to the INEFFIBLE BLESSED STATE OF PURE DIVINE BEINGNESS.

Arjuna said in the second chapter that, 'It is far better for me to live on alms than to get into this battle, wherein I have to do this heinous action, and be a cause to kill all these revered and respected people.' The only person eligible to live on alms is a *sanyasi*, a recluse monk. Therefore he was saying, 'It would be far better for me to renounce life, and live as a *sanyasi*; that is as a contemplative monk.' To that, Krishna is now giving him the answer in explicit terms.

Because Arjuna was a man of the world, very active and had the spirit of a *kshatriya*, that is, one who has a dynamic attitude towards life. He was not only born as a *kshatriya*, but he had the spirit of one too. As a prince, he had all the dynamism and the vitality of life and was in the forefront of social life. Leading an active life and participating in all matters of the world, and was the foremost warrior during his time. For such a person, it would be inappropriate to renounce life, and live quietly on alms as a monk. Just like when you make a dog to sit down and keep quiet, and the moment the dog hears the neighbor's dogs barking, this dog immediately of its own nature gets excited, because that is its nature. As far as Arjuna was concerned, because of his active dynamic nature, whenever trouble is brewing around the corner, do you think he can peacefully sit down? No, his mind will alert to battle the situation. Instinctively he will be drawn into it.

Therefore, for a person like Arjuna, and for people living an active life, their *dharma* is to live in the world and battle the battles of life. So long as a person has desire, ambition, duties, responsibilities, and things to achieve, that person must live in the society, leading an active life. That is his *dharma*. To live in the world and actively participate in the world, becomes a suitable training ground for his own development because that is his appropriate field of action. The appropriate field of a normal man with desires and ambitions is the society around him. The whole of life around you is a field of action in which you are to live and participate. As per one's nature and character one has to live in the world, and thereby get molded and tempered. This is the place where you acquire experience and grow. This is the appropriate earth plane for a normal person to function and live.

Then becoming more specific, *dharma* as we said is determined by three factors. One is the cosmic laws, which are applicable to one and all. Then one has to fit in with the social laws governing a particular society, and then the third and most important factor is one's own *dharma* essentially based on one's nature. Whatever your nature is, as per this is your own *dharma*. That is *svadharma*, one's own *dharma*. As per your tendencies, temperament, and inclination, your *dharma* would be determined.

If a particular person has the character and a strong tendency to take to music, and has the capacity for it and wants to be a musician, then that is the natural character of that person to get into the musical line, and to develop in that field. If such a person were to be put into another line, like medicine, or get into the army that would be alien to the nature of this person, and he would not be happy there. That field would not be conducive for the well-being of this person.

In certain countries, according to one's aptitudes and tendencies, one's course of life is determined. Also one does well in that field in which one has a particular tendency or an inclination. One is also happy there. That becomes natural to the person. If by pressure of society or some other factor, the person were put into another field which is foreign to one's nature, then that becomes *paradharma*, another's *dharma*.

According to society, the social conventions and practices are such that there is a tendency to be this or that. To take to this profession or that. But if they are foreign and alien to your nature, then they will not be conducive to your well-being. Therefore, a person must take to a line of work, which is in accordance with his nature of being.

Human nature is basically psychological and can be classified into various categories. In the Hindu society in India, the so-called caste system, was the basis of classification. This classification was erroneously and mischievously based on the physiology of the individual determined by birth. As things went wrong somewhere in the olden days in the Indian society when the pagan *Brahmin* priests deliberately imposed a false caste system, mischievously invoking Divine sanction for it, in order to exploit the innocence and the good faith of the people and live as social parasites. Instead of it being a psychological classification, the concept degenerated into a physiological consideration which had imbalanced and ruined Indian society. Unfortunately this is what we have today as the Indian setup of the caste system.

In the true psychological classification every society in the world is made up of four groups: *Brahmin*, *Kshatriya*, *Vaisya*, and *Sudra*. These are four psychological classifications based on the nature and the character of a person. Thus the Bhagavad Gita chapter IV, verse 13 mentions. The Gita is a Hindu scripture. It is not even appropriate to call it a Hindu scripture, it is a scripture. As the Bible is not only meant for Christians but is a scripture meant for one and all. Similarly, the scriptures, the Bhagavad Gita and the Upanishads, had their origin in India. Nevertheless their contents are meant for the entire human race. But as per the narrow Indian classification, there is only one way you can be a Hindu, and that is to be born a Hindu, there is no other way. You can only be born a Hindu, and not made a Hindu, as you had to fit into the prevalent fraudulent caste system determined at birth.

The true four-fold classification of the caste system is meant for the entire human race. Since a scripture is not only meant for a localized group of people in a particular geographic area, its contents have a wider application relevant for the entire human race. Therefore this Hindu classification has a broader implication.

As per the true psychological classification, a *Brahmin* is one who in his nature and temper has the preponderance of *sattwa guna*, the mode of serenity in his nature. In such a person a natural dispassion for the material things of the world would be manifest. He would have no worldly desire, ambitions and interests, and would be at peace, wanting nothing, desiring nothing. Also the person who has this nature would naturally have mind control, sense control, and lead an austere life. He would be straightforward, always speaking the truth, and be unconcerned with money. He would be a pure soul, a good being always kind and generous. That is a *sadhu* by nature, which means saintly in disposition. At the same time, his aspirations would be oriented towards the Divine. His main vision would be towards God, and not towards the mythological and pagan gods. A person who has these characteristics, is said to be a *Brahmin* whether he be an Indian, or a Chinese, an African, or a Japanese, or an American. In whichever part of the world he is, any person who has this psychological character within him is said to be a *Brahmin* whether he be a Hindu, Buddhist or Christian, etc. Such a person would be living a quiet spiritual life in prayers and meditation. He would be by nature incapable of any worldly pursuits and professions. In short he would live a contemplative life of a hermit.

This description of who a *Brahmin* is, would only fit some of the holy men in the world, *sadhus* and hermits and some of the nuns and monks of the world, who lead a quiet indrawn contemplative life. For that is the nature of a *Brahmin*, and this concept would never be applicable to people who have just the opposite qualities of greed, passion, anger, hatred, malice, envy, jealousy, pride, arrogance, and who are clever, devious, cunning, and crooked. So it is quite obvious how the prevelent Indian classification determined by birth has done grievous damage to the Hindu society.

Thus the word "*pundit*" means, he whose mind is established in God, who is God-focussed, and not in mundane pursuits of music, arts, science, worldly professions and worldly religio-social rituals. Indian society also calls the *pundit* as *panda*, as one who performs religious rituals.

Thus when a person becomes a true *Brahmin* by nature, he loses interest in all worldly matters, leads a very simple life, with very little needs and wants. This is possible as he ceases to have any further mundane desires, and is now totally focused towards God and Truth. Such a person automatically becomes a hermit or lives like a hermit with no outward show and ostentation.

Also because of his pious, gentle, peaceful, and serene nature, the true *Brahmin* would be meditating on God, and would not be invoking the gods for worldly and material prosperity. Nor would he be capable of entering into any pursuit or activity which is worldly in nature, on account of his *satva* mode of nature.

Then, the character of a person who is a *Kshytriya* is one who has the *rajo guna*, the mode of dynamic activity predominant, along with the *sattwa guna* subordinate to it. The character of such a person is that he has valor, is brave, is an active member of society, very ambitious, wants to do and achieve things, wants to rule and obtain position, power and glory. All these things are the natural characteristics of a person who is a *Kshytriya*. So for him are those worldly pursuits. Most of the people in the world are *Kshatriyas* because this is the normal aspiration of people. They want power, glory, position, and material well-being. For it, they have bravery, and valor, and want to do this and that. Because it is in their own nature. If these *Kshatriyas* who have this nature, were to take to the role of a contemplative *Brahmin*, then what a tragedy would it be! It would well nigh be impossible, because they do not have that character, wherein there is calmness and peace, and is unconcerned of worldly prosperity and worldly well-being. Such a character is something alien and foreign to him, and thereby would be *paradharma*; that is another's *dharma*.

Then we have the third type which is called the *Vaisya*. The *Vaisya* is one who has the character and quality of a businessman who is basically money-minded and wants to engage in trade for it. He has the *rajas* predominant, but instead of the *sattwa*, has the *tamas* subordinate to it. *Tamas* is the mode of inertia. Those people who are acutely money-minded and money-conscious are totally geared towards becoming prosperous through money-making, could be called *Vaisyas*. Agriculture and farming too is included in this category. Those people who get into these professions or occupations for money have this character of a *Vaisya*. In the modern world today people are getting into business. Business is primarily oriented to make money. So all the multi-nationals and the small-nationals are all oriented towards money. Those people have this tendency for making money, in some form or the other. The *Brahmin* priests of India perform religious rituals only for money. Those people who want to become doctors, primarily do so for money. The motive that drives them to be a doctor is the money and not a humanitarian care. That is why it is a medical racket and not a medical care of love and compassion. "No money, no care," is the motto of a doctor. (So the *Brahmin* priests and the doctors are all *Vaisyas* is very clear.)

The fourth character in the society is said to be the *sudras* in the Hindu system. Herein the *tamas*, the mode of inertia is predominant, accompanied with a certain amount of *rajas*. These people get into certain forms of occupation. Thus we find four groups of people classified according to their temperament and nature. If a person were to follow one's own nature or temperament, then that is one's own *dharma, svadharma*. This is how one is to determine and find out what one's own *dharma* is. A *dharma* which is foreign to one's own nature and inclinations is said to be *paradharma*, that is another's *dharma*, to which one is a stranger. Therefore, one should follow one's own *dharma*, based on one's own nature, aptitude and inclination. So one's own character, temperament, and nature of being determine what one's own *dharma* or way of living is, by which one would go about living in the world.

'According to this classification, Arjuna, not only were you raised in the *Kshyatriya* family, but more than that, you have the temper, the character, and the nature of a *Kshyatriya*. Therefore it is your duty to get into this action.' Therefore, he is telling him that one has to understand what one's *dharma* is, and what occupation and way of life one should undertake. Once this is understood, it is easy for one to determine what one's *dharma* in life is going to be. If a person were to live by that, then that person would naturally be happy.

With respect to the *dharma* of one, there is an interesting episode in the Indian epic Mahabharata. Once Bhisma was troubled as to what his *dharma* in life is. As he sat brooding over it, on the bank of the river Ganges, his celestial mother appeared before him and advised him. She said, "What you had resolved to do, namely, 'to assist whoever was the king to rule the kingdom' is your *dharma*, now follow it up, and execute it, for the rest of your life." In the same way, once we have discerned what our *dharma* in life is, then we must follow it up, and live it for the rest of our lives.

Then he says, "*Svadharme nidhanam sreyaha.*" (Even) death in one's *dharma* is better. Once you live your own *dharma* as per your nature, it is far better indeed to die at one's duty, at one's post than to perform another's *dharma*, however well. To die at one's duty is an exalted thing. Therefore he says, 'By living your life in this manner, you are going through your own *dharma* and it is far better to die in it than to perform another's *dharma* which is foreign to one.'

Therefore, we must understand this concept very carefully. Even in a family of four children, each one would have a different temperament and nature. Therefore the *dharma* of each would be different from the other. The wise parent is that who determines and finds out the *sva-dharma* of a particular child, and encourages him in that direction. Then in that field the child would grow up to be happy in the world, and be a happy individual. It is not that just because you are a *Kshyatriya* you put all your children into the army. Or just because you were born in the so-called "*Brahmin*" family, you raise all your children as pagan priests in the *Brahmin* occupation. Certainly not! According to the nature, the *dharma* of the person is.

He says, "*Para dharmo bhayavaha.*" Another's *dharma* is fraught with fear. Because it is foreign to oneself. However well you do that, you do not derive the benefit of it. Since it is not in your nature and therefore are a hypocrite. And thus hypocritically function and live. Thus living and following another's *dharma* does no good to you.

When one follows and lives one's *dharma*, then one is happy in life. Then one lives well and does good to one's well-being. Thereby one flows with the natural flow and rhythm of life. For, remember, having created you, God did not want you to live miserably and unhappily. It is society which has crippled you, and fenced your inner potential.

Then in the next verse, Arjuna is raising a very interesting point. Verse number 36:

****

अथ केन प्रयुक्तोऽयं पापं चरति पूरुषः ।
अनिच्छन्नपि वार्ष्णेय बलादिव नियोजितः ॥ ३६ ॥

Atha kena prayukthoyam paapam carati puurushaha।
Aniccanapi vaarsneya balaadhiva niyojita॥

Oh! Varsneya (Krishna), thus unwillingly and forcibly as it were, impelled by what does a person commit sin?   (36)

****

Arjuna says, 'Krishna, kindly tell me, why individuals are impelled to do wrong things, follow improper course of actions and thereby commit sins and crimes? Because of what do human beings do unrighteous and vicious acts, even though they do not wish to?'

In spite of oneself, one is inexorably driven to commit sins and sinful acts, forceably, as if it were. Just like a master who compels a servant to do something. What is that which forces people to commit crimes and wrong deeds? What impels and makes them do all those vicious deeds? Even though people know well what they are doing is wrong, nevertheless, in spite of themselves, inexorably are driven to do it. There is a strong force within which makes them do things, as if forcibly. They don't even think twice about it, even though they know it is wrong.

In the city of New York, or for that matter in any city, if the lights went off during the whole night, you would find all the stores smashed and looted in a few hours. The opportunity comes, and within a few hours, all the showcases are broken open. For, there is an energy operating within each, which impels one into whatever action. What makes people do these things? They know well that what they are going to do is wrong. To this, the reply is given by Krishna.

In verse number 37 he says:

****

काम एषः क्रोध एषः रजोगुणसमुद्भवः ।
महाशनो महापाप्मा विद्धयेनमिह वैरिणम् ॥ ३७ ॥

Kaama esha krodha esha rajogunasamudbhavaha।
Mahasano mahapapma viddhyenamiha vairinam।।

It is desire, it is anger arising out of the *rajo guna* (mode of nature) insatiable, the great sinner which is the enemy here.   (37)

****

That which makes people do wrong and sinful acts, is nothing but desire and anger. "*Kaama esa krodha esa.*" *Kaama* means a very strong, inordinate desire. A powerful passionate urge in a person. The person is burning with desire and is in the heat of it and has a compelling urge to fulfill it. If a man passes by a sweet-shop and on seeing the sweets even though is diabetic, buys it. That strong urge to do so is said to be this *kaama*, desire.

It is this impulsive force within a person which makes him do heinous and wrong things. Thus when the desire is unfulfilled, one is sad, uncomfortable, and is burning with desire. And when the desire is obstructed, it transfers into anger, *krodha*. If some person becomes an obstruction to that desire, or to the fulfillment of that desire, immediately that same desire transforms itself into *krodha*, anger. That same desire manifests itself now as anger. And once you get angry, you act in ways that you wouldn't have thought of doing before.

When a person is in these two states, he is beside himself.

He is not subject to reason at that time. All reason deserts him. When a person is in this intense state of desire and also is in an intense state of anger, then at that moment, all good sense and discrimination leave him. That is why when you are angry, you wouldn't hesitate even to scold your teacher, or abuse your parents. Even the wife will speak harshly to the husband, and the husband will talk harshly to the wife in unbecoming language in strong hateful words. And the children likewise talk in that manner, to their elders. Anger is such a vicious thing, as when the anger subsides, you repent what you had said, or done before. In anger you do things and say things which you normally would not have done. Anger destroys one and others too.

When anger is in that person, his eyes become bloodshot, and if he has a mustache, it begins to twitch, and the blood gushes to his brain. There are two cities in Madras state in India called Madurai and Mana Madurai at a distance of thirty miles apart. It was said that one person got a blow from another person in Madurai, but his mustache twitched in anger only in Mana Madurai, thirty miles away. His anger was there, but he dare not show it, lest he get another blow. So he went thirty miles away, and there his mustache was twitching with anger. And he was saying, "If I see that man, what will I do with him?" These are the characteristics of an angry person. Also, the angry person cannot stand still, he begins to vibrate.

When a person is angry, there are two things that happen to him. Either he becomes an eloquent orator, or begins to stutter. Because he is so angry either the words cannot come out of his mouth, or on the other hand, he is so angry that even a passive man would be an eloquent speaker. Torrents of words would be coming out of him. See what anger does to a person? That is the character of anger.

Desire is less manifest than anger. But in order to obtain the desires, the person will do anything. When the person is burning with desire he will be prepared to sell all his possessions for it. It makes a man lose all good reason.

Therefore he says, *kaama* (desire), and *kroda* (anger), can ruin a person. Once the words gush out of your mouth in anger, you cannot take them back. They have done their damage. Once you have broken a watch, at the most you can mend it, but the joint is still there. So too the scar of anger is there. It sears the heart of another. Therefore, one must be very careful not to be a victim of these two.

Further he says, they arise out of *rajas* - *rajo guna samudbhavaha*. The three *gunas* of nature are: *satva* (serenity), *rajas* (dynamism), and *tamas* (inertia.) When *rajas* mode of nature operates, aggressiveness comes into the person. Thus desire and anger arise out of the *rajas* mode of nature. That is one meaning. The other is these two also give rise to *rajas*. The first meaning is these two come out of *rajo guna*. Desire and anger come out of *rajas guna*. If a person does not have the *rajo guna* in him, then he will not have this inordinate anger or desire. But because there is the *rajo guna* in him, therefore, these two come out of his nature. The reverse is also true. The moment desire comes in, *rajo guna* arises. The moment there is anger, immediately the *rajas* state is also manifested. Thus, in both sense, it either comes out of *rajo guna*, or it brings about the *rajo guna*.

Therefore, in order to overcome your *rajo guna*, and be in a *sattwic* state of serenity and calmness, what should you do? If you can overcome your desire patterns and deal with your anger, then that state of *rajo guna* of emotional imbalance will not transpire. The solution to the problem is to overcome your own nature, riddled with desires, and anger. Thereby that which brings about the *rajo guna* will not be. Thus will you overcome *rajo guna*, by overcoming anger and desire.

All of you know well that anger can always be controlled. Often people say, "I was an angry man, in past tense." It is a common statement. And you know what has happened to him? By living in the world, the world has tempered him. Often his wife and children temper him. By living in the world, man gets so frustrated, and scratches his head in sheer exasperation as to what to do in life. He gets molded and tempered in course of time. It happens to both man and woman. Thus you find in course of time, as the years go by, you begin to overcome your anger. It is more under control now.

So also with desires too. In your young days, you had so many desires. You can make a big list of them. But as you grow older, you become the wiser for it, and realize the futility of entertaining desires. You are now content with whatever you have, as you are getting tempered by living life. The secret of living a happy life, is to be content with whatever providence brings you in life. Thus as a result the intensity of the *rajo guna* is less.

This desire is such a great eater. However much you feed it, it is never satisfied, it never feels full. A person may be a glutton, and you give him all the food that he wants. His stomach is full, and for the moment he is satisfied, but in a few hours he is craving once again. Within a few hours he demands more and more. The next day also it is the same thing. The craving never stops for a gluttonous person. That desire cannot ever be fulfilled, though he eat every day.

Desire has that character. Today you have a desire for this, and you satisfy this desire. But the next day another arises. First you come to the United States with a few dollars. Thereafter, you buy an old second-hand car and drive that around. Later on, you buy a new small car because there is a desire for it. And then you wind up with a big new car. Thereafter you buy an expensive big car. Even then you are not satisfied. Even if you become the

191

president, the satisfaction will not be there. Thus desires keep on multiplying, and one cannot be at peace. That is why it is called *mahashana* - the great eater, the great consumer. The more you fulfill your desires, the more and more it wants. It doesn't say it is enough. The feeling of being enough is never there. So it is called the *mahashana*, the great eater.

Because it cannot be satiated, it is called the *mahaa paapma* - the great sinner. It is a great sinner, because it cannot be satiated. You cannot ever satisfy your desires. That is it's very nature. It is insatiable. It goes on and on within you. Today you have this, tomorrow you need that, the day after you need something else. It goes on and on, and is a never-ending process. It compounds itself. As you get more and more money, you realize you have more and more expenses. Everything increases. Later on, you may come to such a point in order to fulfill the desires, the person may do wrong things, in order to obtain the desires. He may use wrong means and methods. So what makes a man do crimes, wrong deeds, and heinous acts? It is desire which makes a person commit all errors and crimes.

Viddhi enam iha vairinam. Thus this desire is the great enemy of man. So long as desire exists strong, it is the foremost enemy for a person. One's own desire is one's own biggest enemy. Because it will not allow you to be in peace. The lesser the desire, the more peace you have. If perchance you have no desires, you are the most peaceful man in the world. What makes you drive into activity? What makes you plunge headlong into the world? It is nothing but your desires. Impelled by these desires you plunge headlong to fulfill them. From morning to evening you are prepared to undergo all the difficulties and miseries, just to fulfill them. Therefore, it is something which is insatiable by nature. This is what causes all the errors in man.

Then Krishna asks, 'In what manner does this desire come and obstruct a person's good understanding?'

The next verse, 38:

****

धूमेनाव्रियते वह्निर्यथादर्शो मलेन च ।
यथोल्बेनावृतो गर्भस्तथा तेनेदमावृतम् ॥ ३८ ॥

Dhumenavriyete vanniryathadarso malena ca|
yatholbenavrito garbastatha tenedamavritam||

Just as the fire is covered or obscured by the smoke; just as the mirror is covered by dust; just as the fetus is covered by the womb, in the same way too, this is covered by that (desire).   (38)

****

The word "this" is discussed in the next verse. Three classic examples have been given here. Where there is fire, the smoke is around it. Even though the smoke is around the fire, and covers and obscures it, nevertheless, a little of the fire is always visible. If you fan the fire, naturally, the smoke goes away. The fire becomes visible and manifest. By a mere fanning, the smoke goes away and the fire blazes. This could be compared to the veil of the *sattva guna* mode of nature which obscures slightly.

Every person has three *gunas*, the *sattva guna*, the *rajo guna*, and *tamo guna*. In each one of the three *gunas* there is a corresponding veil. In the *sattva guna*, the veil is very light, it is a subtle, light veil. Just with a little breeze, the smoke curling around the fire goes away. The fire becomes manifest, and blazes more. The veil of the *sattva guna* is just like the veil of the smoke which can be quickly fanned away. So too also with the removal of the subtle psychological impurities, the person will be able to perceive the Truth of life.

193

The second example is that of the mirror covered by a great deal of dust and encrustation. It requires a little bit of scrubbing and cleaning to cleanse the mirror. Naturally then you will be able to see the reflection. This is like the *rajo guna* in a person. The three *gunas* are there in every person veiling his God-nature. Only thing is that their proportion is different. With a little bit of cleansing over a small period of time, you will be able to get over the *rajo guna* veil.

Then comes the third example of the veil. Just like the fetus in the abdomen is covered by the womb. It totally covers it, and you are unable to see the little child because the covering is very dense now. It is so dense that the formation of the child cannot be seen by the naked eyes. The hands, the feet, the face and the features of the child, or whether it is a boy or a girl is not visible. You are unable to distinguish because it has been covered. This is just like the *tamo guna* veil in a person. Thus the *tamo guna* veil is a little more dense. It obscures any penetration of light. Light means an intelligent understanding or awareness. The heavy density and intense dullness of the mind is the *tamo guna* veil. Thus by that strong desire, this good understanding is obscured, is the import of this verse.

Verses 39 - 43

Lord Krishna was answering a question put forward by Arjuna, as to what causes people to get into wrong and unrighteous deeds, and sinful activities, in spite of their better sense. Knowing the consequences and the implications of whatever they do, inexorably people do many a wrong act and deed.

Therefore, he is asking Krishna what is that force which makes people do this? Lord Krishna beautifully replies, 'The basic cause of it is *kaama* - desire.' And the very same desire transforms itself into anger, when the desire is thwarted and thereby wreaks havoc in the lives of people. It is desire which impels people into various forms of activities in the world, and causes wrong deeds too. Therefore it is this which has to be controlled and overcome.

Basically, a person's approach to life is impelled by two factors - likes and dislikes. On account of likes and impelled by his own desires, a person engages in activities, and also gets away from activities which he doesn't want to do, if perchance he dislikes them. It seems as if *raga* and *dwesha*, likes and dislikes, seem to be very powerful motive forces for all actions in the world.

In overcoming these two factors, *raga* and *dwesha*, one is in a position thereby to rise above one's natural instinctive nature. The Lord said that if one subjects oneself to the higher law of life, as revealed and taught by me (Krishna), and the other great teachers too, then one rises above not only the likes and dislikes, but also rises above desire, too. Therefore he says that this is the way by which we can rise above our own nature, and thereby not be victimized by it.

Thereafter he spoke about desires which bring havoc in the

lives of people, and as long as people have desires in their nature, they would be tormented individuals. What goes to torment you in life is your own desire patterns. When you are free of your desires, you are totally free and happy. Then at that time a state of peace permeates your mind. Thus it is desires which make you do things in the world. In order to obtain and fulfill them, they impel you to do many things. Therefore he says, 'This desire is the greatest foe in man.' The desire to do this, achieve this, and obtain that.

Various forms of desire come to a person. Thus a person is nothing but an embodiment of desire itself - *kaama mayo purusha*. The *word kaama* is even stronger in sense than the English word desire. It is an inordinate, strong compelling urge to possess or have something. The passion for it. That is what is understood by the word *kaama*. When desire comes to a person, and he is unable to fulfill that particular *kaama* or strong urge and passion, then for that moment the person is in a state of unease till he obtains and fulfills it. Moreover this strong impulse in a person covers his good sense too. It veils all good sense and understanding, which a person is capable of living by.

Krishna said, 'It is by that strong impulse called *kaama*, desire, this is veiled.' In the next verse, he is going to very precisely pinpoint and tell you what he means by "this."

Verse 39:

****

आवृतं ज्ञानमेतेन ज्ञानिनो नित्यवैरिणा ।
कामरूपेण कौन्तेय दुष्पूरेणानलेन च ॥ ३९ ॥

Aavritam jnnanametena jnnanino nityavairinaa।
Kaamarupena kaunteya duspurenanalena ca॥

196

Oh Kaunteya (Arjuna), like the insatiable fire, this desire obscures as a constant enemy, the knowledge-awareness of the wise. (39)

****

He explains here, what is meant by the word "this" in the previous verse. For Lord Krishna had said earlier, desire veils and covers "this." In the subject under discussion, the word *itam* here stands for knowledge, or discriminative understanding. To be more precise, it stands for the state of discriminative awareness. The mind state of discrimination. Having lived in the world, you arrive at an understanding that there is something more to life than what immediately appears. Therefore, you seek to obtain an awareness of that Reality which is beyond empirical life. Is there something which is the reality of existence, the truth of life? In course of time you will come to understand what the truth of life is, through the teachings of the scriptures, and through the teachings of the wise. For, the scripture talks to you about the truth of life.

It would be very strange for a modern educated man to even understand that the truth of life has already been known, discovered, and understood by the wise all over the world. The modern educated mind finds it difficult to even comprehend this. He is very much oriented towards the Western type of education. In modern science, they are still trying to discover what the truth is, and they have very few clues about it. But herein we find that the great mystics, from time to time, have revealed to mankind, what the truth of life is all about. That is the truth revealed in the scriptures. The scriptures declare to you what the truth is, and what the untruth and false is. This knowledge pertaining to the Truth of life is very clearly revealed in the scripture. Thus it is that knowledge and its awareness which we are talking about.

Once you have obtained that knowledge, or rather, when

your time comes, when you are ready to receive this knowledge, appreciate it and live by it, then by Divine Grace that knowledge opens out to you. Rather, you open yourself to that knowledge. Until then, till you are ready, that knowledge remains a closed book, as far as you are concerned. You receive that knowledge only when you become ready for it psychologically and mentally. Thus when you mature in life, you open out on account of that maturity to receive the higher wisdom and knowledge. Then on account of the fact that you are opening up in your own mind, and when you look around, then you receive that knowledge. Blessed are the people, who have this good fortune to so open their minds and receive this knowledge, understand and appreciate it, and thereafter, live by it. Therefore, when the time comes you receive it.

Therefore what should people seek for? They should seek for the good teachings. It is the good teachings which will free and liberate them. Instead they seek for the so-called *gurus*, and super-*gurus*, and adulate and worship them as if that is the panacea for all their ills of life.

This knowledge talks about what the reality, the ultimate truth of life is. It also reveals to you what is not the truth, and is false. Once this becomes clear, then all you have to do is try to maintain your awareness in this understanding. That is, try to maintain your conscious-awareness in the truth of life, which has been revealed. The act of doing so, is undertaken in meditation. Thus meditation is the simple act of maintaining Truth-Awareness. It involves no initiation, but only a Truth teaching and instruction.

It says very clearly, that the total essence of that knowledge is the Divine, the only reality. In the Hindu scriptures *Brahman* is the word used for the Reality. That Divine Reality also happens to be your essential nature. In your essential nature, every one is the Divine, the Divinity in existence. In the state of being as the Divine one is full, perfect, and self-complete in all sense.

Thus once you get to appreciate the truth, then all you have to do is, maintain your conscious awareness in this truth of life, which happens to be your essential nature. All that you have to do now, is to maintain the state of discriminative awareness. Discrimination always implies two things. One is the real, the other is the false. Knowing the truth as the truth, and false as the unreal. The unreal is the false. Thereafter you have the good sense and wisdom, born of conviction and appreciation, to maintain your conscious-awareness in the real. For which you have the moral and spiritual strength called as soul force - *atma bal*, to shift your awareness from the false, and focus it on the real. This process is the application of intelligence. When you are so able to focus on the real, by shifting your awareness from the unreal which hitherto had held your attention, then that particular character or tendency which you have acquired now is said to be *viveka*, the state of discrimination or discriminative awareness. This is called wisdom, or living by the higher truth.

Having understood the higher truth and thereby living your life in that awareness, in religious parlance is called as living in God-awareness or maintaining God-consciousness. It is the tendency or capacity or the effort you make to maintain your awareness in the reality.

Let not the word "God" bewilder or frighten you. Truth is the Reality in Existence. That is why it is real, as it always exists for all times. Therefore it is true, and is the Truth. This Truth has to be conscious of its beingness. Therefore, in religious parlance it is called as God. So the word God means the Self-conscious Truth of Life, or the Truth of all life which pervades and permeates all that which is, as its inherent life principle. This life principle is alive or rather to be more precise, awake to its beingness. Thus do not imagine that the word God means, a being sitting yonder somewhere as a physical entity. Therefore when you too become alive or awake to this inherent principle within, it is referred to as God experience or Truth experience. That is experiencing the Truth of your God-nature within. And God-nature means the perfected state of beingness, which is self-complete, one and whole. Therefore it is also referred as the "Blessed State" - Shiva padam.

At the present moment, your awareness is totally involved in the universe and in the objects and things of the world. Therefore, having understood what the truth is, you tend to lift your awareness from the things of the world and make an effort to maintain your conscious-awareness in the Divine, which is your essential nature. Later on at the end of this chapter, Lord Krishna will tell you how to maintain your awareness in your own essential nature. To so do and experience your Divine nature is the goal of life.

But in the living of life you get preoccupied and carried away by desire, it does not allow you to maintain this state of discriminative awareness. This is its very character, and robs your attention like a thief. It carries you away, kidnaps and holds you at ransom. It takes you away from the reality, and makes you preoccupied with its own fulfillment. Thus, this *kaama* (desire), obscures, and covers you from your reality and also from trying to maintain this state of discriminative awareness of it.

Therefore he says, '*kaama* is the eternal foe of the wise who are attempting to maintain the state of discrimination.' Certainly it is not a foe for the unwise. The unwise do not care about it. They are quite content in their worldly pursuits, and in getting entangled in the world. So for the unregenerate, the unwise who have not been educated in this knowledge, this *kaama* is not a foe. They are quite comfortable and happy with it. But it is a foe only for the spiritual seeker of truth.

When desire comes, the individual is nothing but a mass of desire, a personification of it. He transforms himself into an all-consuming passion. Similarly, when a man becomes angry, he is all anger, a personification of anger. You might say he is a mass of anger. Desire is equally like that. The person becomes a personification of desire.

Lord Krishna is addressing Arjuna, as the son of Kunthi. He says, 'This desire is insatiable. It can never by satisfied, or fulfilled.' It makes its demand over and over again. Fire consumes everything. The more materials you put into the fire, its demand is inexhaustible. If you keep on pouring ghee or clarified butter into the fire, it burns brightly, even more gloriously consuming everything in its way. Even if it dies down a little, once again if you put in a little more, it further ignites and glows. This aspect of fire is ever insatiable. That is why the word *mahaashana* has been used. It means never enough. The more and more you put into it, the more and more it ignites and glows more brilliantly.

Therefore, *kaama*, desire, is like this fire. The scriptures declare that the desires cannot be overcome by further indulging in them. The more and more you indulge, the more strongly you get involved in it, and get carried away by it. That is not the way to overcome them. The more you give into it, the more you want to allow these desires to manifest and take roots in you. It becomes more and more. Never by giving into it, does one get over it.

But then, how is a person able to overcome desire? The technique to overcome desire is revealed in the next three verses, which are the concluding verses of this chapter. It says beautifully how one could overcome this desire, however strong it is. The first thing that you have to know is, that desire is the enemy of man, not of all man, but of discriminative men. Then you must know where it is located. Where its *asraya* is. Where does it reside? If you know the abode of your enemy, then perhaps you will be able to deal with him and tackle him. In the next verse, where it resides in a human individual is very nicely revealed.

****

इन्द्रियाणि मनोबुद्धिरस्याधिष्ठानमुच्यते ।
एतैर्विमोहयत्येष ज्ञानमावृत्य देहिनम् ॥ ४० ॥

Indriyani mano buddhirasyadhistananmuchate|
Ethyirvimohayatyesha jnanamaavritya dehinam||

This (desire) resides in the senses, mind and the intellect. Having covered the knowledge-awareness through them it deludes the embodied (soul). (40)

****

Desire resides at three places. It first of all abides in the ten senses. Man has ten senses: the five sense organs of knowledge, and the five sense organs of action. The five sense organs of knowledge are the sense of sight, the sense of hearing, touch, taste and the sense of smell. It is with which you receive knowledge and information from the world. The five organs of action are the hands, feet, the organ of speech, reproduction and the organ of evacuation with which you come in contact with the world. Thus these are the ten sense organs, wherein desire resides.

Desire resides in the mind, too. Even when you are shut in a dark room, or when you are all by yourself with nothing to do, the desire is in the mind. You begin to entertain the desireful thoughts there.

In the *buddhi* too, the desire resides. *Buddhi* means the intellect. What is the distinction between the mind and the intellect? The mind is that which constantly vacillates, from thought to thought, being involved with its thought patterns. Now it thinks of this, thereafter it thinks of that. The buddhi, the intellect is that which decides, makes a definite decision. "This is how it is." "This is the particular thing I want." It is one and the same mind, when it plays the part of making a decision, is called the intellect. Having analyzed many things, then it decides exactly what it wants, what it desires.

Therefore, intellect, is also the abode for desire, just as the mind is. The mind keeps on thinking, and desiring many things. So do the senses too. The moment you open your eyes and see the form world around you, you immediately desire that which is pleasing to you, if it is in your proximity. That is why it is dangerous to go to the mall. The merchants also know this, that is why they display the goods, so that the moment you see it, desire immediately comes spontaneously. A woman wants to stand in front of the display of *saris*, but the man wants to drag her away before desire takes root in her mind through the senses. So they have a tug-of-war there. In the mind too, the desire patterns keep on coming. It is constantly there. Thirdly, it is in the intellect because once you have made the decision, that is a fatal error. Until then, the senses have seen it, the mind is deliberating over it, but the moment you make the fatal decision, "yes I need it," you are finished. The intellect is the third place where desire resides, and that is the dangerous part, because that gives the decision to go ahead. Thus it resides in the intellect too. So the abode of *kaama*, which is a stronger word than desire, resides in the senses, the mind, and the intellect.

Residing there, what does it do? By residing in these three places it deludes a person. Desire fools and confounds him. This desire is born of ignorance of your essential nature. The moment you are born into this world in a physical body with a mind, you come to realize that you are a human being. Thus, you experience in yourself a feeling of inadequacy, and incompleteness as a human being. Why is it? Because the original error is ignorance. You have forgotten your true glorious nature of your being, as the Divine. In your essential nature, you were and are the Divine - the *Atman*. As the Divine, you are perfect and complete. But now, you have this self-forgetfulness. Therefore, God-realization means self-realization, realizing your true nature as the Divine. You have forgotten it, that is self-evident in everyone. It is a natural experience.

Therefore, out of this ignorance, the next step follows. You feel that you are inadequate and incomplete. Thus in order to complete your being, you entertain desires. So desires naturally come to you. You feel that with the desires you will be more complete. Hence in order to fulfill the desires, you get into action. Therefore, this is called the *hridaya granthi*; the knots of the heart. Ignorance, desire, and action. Ignorance and desire lead to action. These three are called the knot of life, by which we are knotted into this empirical universe. Therefore, it is this desire, which covers *viveka* or the discriminative knowledge that you have. For a human being, this desire comes and veils his sense of discrimination from the truth of his own being.

Therefore, how do you overcome this desire, so that you will be able to abide in your own true nature, realize the Divine, and experience the glory of your own being as perfect and full? That is the unconscious aspiration of every single creature. Once you have gained this enlightened understanding, that unconscious urge or aspiration now becomes a conscious effort on your part. Hence learn to abide in your own true nature.

How does one overcome this desire? That technique is revealed in the next three verses. In the first he says:

****

तस्मात्त्वमिन्द्रियाण्यादौ नियम्य भरतर्षभ ।
पाप्मानं प्रजहि ह्येनं ज्ञानविज्ञाननाशनम् ॥ ४१ ॥

Tasmatvamindriyanyadau niyamya bharatarishabha
Papmaanam prajahi heyenam jnanavijnananasanam

Therefore Arjuna, (Bhaarata Rishaba) having controlled the senses
first overcome the sinner which destroys knowledge-awareness and
its experience. (41)
****

Arjuna comes from an illustrious dynasty, therefore he is
called *Bhaarata*. His forefathers were eminent persons. 'Thus it is
not beyond you,' Lord Krishna said, 'because your forefathers had
conquered and ruled this country. Hence you too are no ordinary
mortal. Your forefathers subdued their enemies, you too are capable
of subduing your enemies. And what is your enemy here? It is
kaama (desire) only. Desire is your enemy here. You are a capable,
strong and brave person, who can overcome himself.' Therefore,
Lord Krishna says, 'Since you are foremost amongst men, you are
capable of subduing *kaama*.' Thus he gave him inspiration.

People imagine it is impossible to overcome desire. No, it is
not so. Therefore, what should one do? First of all, in order to
conquer desire, begin controlling the senses. That is why all religions
of the world have enjoined this: to have self-control and the control
of the senses. You must be able to control the senses, and discipline
them whenever you see something captivating, and enticing.
Immediately withdraw your perceptions before they can get through
your senses into your mind and take root therein. What happens is,
if you see something desirable, you immediately desire it. While if
you do not see, you do not. For that moment, desire does not rush
in. But the moment you see, it immediately floods your mind; then
you desire and want it. But if perchance you do not see, then that
desire does not enter the mind. Therefore, it is very wisely said that
first of all, you should control your senses and thereby do not permit

these sense-impresssions to come. But that alone is not sufficient. Thereafter in the mental plane too, as you are seated quietly, desire thoughts come. From the moment these desire thoughts come into your mind, if you allow them free rein, then they begin to take roots in the mind. That is something which every one knows. Therefore, whenever the desire thoughts come, at that moment itself nip it off. You know that if you allow it to take root in your mind, and allow the desire patterns to take over your mind, it is going to take hold of your mind. It is going to overpower your mind. Thus even before that, as it comes, you nip it. You just do not allow it. You say, "This is not a desirable thing because this will lead me to problems." Therefore, you nip it in the mind itself.

That which gives a direction to the mind is the intellect. It is the intellect which gives direction to the mind and says, no. Even though the desires come, it is not desirable. Therefore, beginning from your senses, the mind, and the intellect, you can in turn control each and all of them, one by one, as it manifests. Thus you control the senses, and the mind with the intelligence of the intellect. Also you are going to subject the intellect to live by the higher law of life. You are not going to permit yourself to live as per the old baser ways of living.

Also, all of you know very well, these desires have always tormented you. All through your life they have sought their fulfillment at all times, and have tormented you. Therefore, you know that their presence in you is not very desirable, and you want to get out of it, and be free of it. Once you realize this, you will want to get out of it, and be free of it. Thus the compelling need to get out of desire patterns should first arise in the mind.

Then the second thing is, you must understand that your blessed state is your Divine state. Thus in order to realize it you are constrained to overcome desire. So long as these desires are strongly ingrained in you, you will not be in a position to attain your blessed state. Just as a young student at the college knows that he has to get through his Masters degree, and in order to do that, he has to sacrifice. He has to go through his studies and sacrifice many other indulgences. If he gives in to them, he will not be able to get into his studies and pass his examination. Thus there is sacrifice here. Here too in order to realize your Divine state, some degree of sacrifice is needed. Realizing this with your own intellect, you decide not to permit the desires to take roots in the mind.

Beginning with your senses, you begin to control them. Then through the mind and the intellect, you will be able to overcome desire, which leads you to *papa* or sin. Out of desire, people do sinful things. That which they should not do, they do. The word sinner is used here to refer to "desire." "May you overcome the great sinner called desire." Get it out of your system. This desire is said to be the destroyer of discriminative knowledge referred to by the word *jnaanam* here.

What type of knowledge? The knowledge which you obtain from the scriptures: that there is a Divinity in existence, and that is your essential nature. This definite knowledge which you obtain about yourself through the instructions, is said to be *jnaanam* here. But even though you obtain this knowledge, you have not yet experienced yourself as the Divine. Therefore, *vijnanam* here means special knowledge. The scriptural text-book knowledge is mental or intellectual knowledge and understanding. Through a spiritual life, of meditation, this has to be transformed or translated into an immediate experience of "I am the Divine." That is called *vigjnanam*. Therefore, desire, *kaama*, destroys both *jnaanam*, discriminative awareness as well as the immediate experience, *vigjnanam* too. The word *jnaanam* stands for, that state of discriminative awareness that you are trying to maintain. Having understood that false is false, you are now trying to maintain your awareness in the truth. That tendency or the effort that you are making to maintain your awareness in the truth the *Atman* is said to be *jnaanam* here. It should be noted that *gnanam* does not mean, a mere intellectual grasp. For, once grasped, *kaama* (desire), cannot destroy it. But what *kaama* does is, it prevents and obstructs you from maintaining the state of discriminative awareness, *gnanam*. Thus only it destroys *gnanam*.

Professional preachers, and professional pundits of course have an intellectual grasp of this scriptural knowledge, but on account of their desires, and worldly nature, are unable to maintain this state of discriminative awareness. To do so one requires spiritual virtues and the purity of mind and the purity of heart. Then *gnanam* becomes a living force in one's life, and transforms itself into *vigjnanam*, that is immediate experience. Thus it is in this sense that *kaama* destroys *gnana* and *vigjnanam*.

Or *jnaanam* also means spiritual discernment of the Truth from the false. While *vigjnanam* means the special capacity of the mind to maintain Truth-Awareness in a meditative state. Thus this *kaama* blocks or obstructs both the state of *jnaana* truth knowledge and *vigjnana* (meditative state) transpiring in the mind.

He is now going to reveal a technique to get into the state of meditative awareness, the technique to abide in your own true self. In order to understand this technique, a basic theoretical knowledge is necessary.

****

इन्द्रियाणि पराण्याहुरिन्द्रियेभ्यः परं मनः ।
मनसस्तु परा बुद्धियों बुद्धेः परतस्तु सः ॥ ४२ ॥

Indriyani paranyahurindriyepyaha param manaha|
Manasastu para buddhiryo buddheha paratastu saha||

The senses are said to be superior; the mind is superior to the senses; the *buddhi* (intellect) is superior to the mind; that which is beyond (superior) to the intellect is the *Atman*.   (42)

****

It is said the senses are superior. To what? He has not mentioned it, but your ten senses are superior to the body and to the sense-objects which they reveal. Why is it that they are superior to the body? The senses are more internal than the body. The body is more gross, it is inert, it is localized. The senses are capable of giving you illumination. They are capable of revealing something to you, therefore, they are more luminous than the body which is gross. Therefore, they are superior. The body is limited in its form. The senses have a wider scope of activity. Therefore, they are said to be superior. The senses are said to be more interior than the body. Even if the body is injured, it is only an injury to some part of the body. But if there is an injury to the eyes or to the ears, or to any one of the sense organs, you are more sensitive about it, because they are more interior, than the physical body. For these reasons, the ten sense organs are said to be superior to the body.

Indriyepyaha param manaha. The mind is superior to the senses. As the mind directs the senses to function, the mind is more internal than the sense organs. That is the first reason. The second is, the mind is more subtle than the sense organs. Thirdly, if not for the mind, the messages received by the sense organs have no use. They do not get registered. What gives the sense organs the ability to receive their various sense impressions or sense data? Only when the mind gets attached to them. The mind is able to deal with all the ten sense organs, and receive messages from all of them. Therefore, the mind is superior to the sense organs, and more luminous than the sense organs.

If the mind is not attached to any one of the senses, then you do not receive that information. If your attention is on a good novel, even when someone is calling you, you do not hear. Your mind is focused on the novel intensely, therefore, it is not able to hear, even though the ears are not blocked. When your mind is elsewhere, when it is in deep contemplation, even though the eyes see, it does not get registered. Therefore, the mind is superior to the senses, and it is also said to be more luminous. That is why you are able to perceive things better with the mind. With each sense you only perceive a minute thing, but with the mind you are able to perceive better. The mind is more luminous, more *prakasa* is there. Thus the mind is superior.

Manasastu para buddhi: that which is superior to the mind is said to be the *buddhi*, the intellect. Without the command of the intellect, the mind cannot get into any functions. The mind can get into functions only when the intellect gives it a command to go ahead and think like this, or go ahead and do this. Therefore, the intellect is superior because it has the capacity to give the order to the mind. So the intellect has the power of discrimination. It imposes its command upon the mind. Even when the mind begins to think loose thoughts, the intellect says, "Don't have those thoughts. Don't think like that." Therefore, the intellect is superior to the mind.

Then he says, 'There is one thing which is superior to the intellect.' *Buddher paratastu saha*. "This" is superior to the intellect. The word *saha* - this, here stands for the *Atman*, which is there within you. Or rather which is you. When we use the word *Atman*, it means your real nature, your essential nature as the Divine. The *Atman* is *Brahman*, the truth of life, and that is superior to the intellect.

How is it superior to the intellect? The mind is inert, but it seems to be luminous. It seems to obtain luminosity from the *Atman*. We could compare the mind to a pool of water, and the *Atman* to the moon or the sun. When there is a pool of water, and the sun or the moon is up in the sky, immediately you see the reflected sun or the moon. There is a reflection in the pool. That same moon is not reflected in the earth around the water. The water has the capacity to reflect, but not the earth. The earth is denser. Even though both are matter, water is a water element, the earth is an earth element. The reflection is possible only in the water element, not in the earth element.

Similarly also, the reflection of the original consciousness which is the *Atman*, is possible in the mind, but not in the body. The body is more gross, denser, while the mind's in-built character is a little luminous and has the capacity to reflect the original consciousness. The original light is the light of the sun or the moon. That is why in the pool of water, you are able to see the moon. The moon is full, and in the moonlight you can see things. You can see the moon in the water but not in the earth. Similarly, the mind's in-built character is luminous. Therefore, you are able to obtain the reflection of the original source, and that is the consciousness of the *Atman*. The mind by its nature is an evolute of nature, it is inert. Nature around you too is inert. Even though the mind is subtle in character, it too, is inert. Nevertheless it has the capacity to have luminosity on account of the reflected consciousness in it. On account of that consciousness, the mind appears to be luminous. You are able to perceive with the mind. You are able to perceive and know that they are thoughts, desires, and inclinations. All these patterns which transpire in the mind, you are able to see in your own consciousness, because of the presence of the original consciousness, the *Atman*.

Even when there are no thought patterns and when the mind is calm, still and quiet, still the awareness of such a still state is always there. This general awareness is always ever present and constant.

It never ceases. With thoughts, or without thoughts, it is always there.

The only thing is, when there are thoughts or visual perceptions, the consciousness therein is more intense. This is because a double consciousness is operating now. One, the original pure consciousness of the *Atman*, and the other its reflected consciousness in the mind. Thus when the mind functions or rather transpires, then the double consciousness occurs. At other moments only the pure consciousness of the *Atman* is present which is general, indistinct, and dim. It being so, that is why you always want to escape into thoughts and perceptions, which is more intense because now the double consciousness is operative.

Thus the luminosity of the mind is due to the presence in it of the reflected consciousness, which in turn derives its luminous power from the original pure consciousness of the *Atman*.

Even when you go to sleep and have a beautiful experience of a dream, in whose light do you experience the entire dream universe? Where has the light come from, for you to see all the things that you see in the dream? In the waking world, if the moon is not there on a dark night, or if you are put into a dark room, you cannot see anything. But you begin to grope your way with the light of your consciousness. But when you are in a dream state, your universe is lived in your mind. All the objects in the dream universe are all lit by the consciousness. That consciousness lights up the whole panorama of life. That consciousness which is self luminous is said to be superior to the mind. That is the *Atman* which one has to realize. That is said to be superior to the intellect. That is the true seer. Anything which is other than the seen is the seer. Anything that is other than you is the seen. That is why you say, "my" intellect, "my" ego. Because you are able to see the intellect functioning, and how it comes to decide. Thus whatever you see is other than you, is different from you. Therefore, this consciousness is said to be superior and beyond the intellect, too. That is said to be the *Atman*.

The next verse:

****

एवं बुद्धे: परं बुद्ध्वा संस्तभ्यात्मानमात्मना ।
जहि शत्रुं महाबाहो कामरूपं दुरासदम् ॥ ४३ ॥

*Evam buddhehe param buddhuva samstabhiyatmanamatmana*l
*Jahi shatrum mahabhaho kaamarupam durasadam*ll

Thus having known that which is superior to the intellect, establish the mind (in the *Atman*) with the intellect.
Thus should you conquer the enemy of desire, difficult to overcome.
(43)

****

Having understood and known that there is this *Atman* that is beyond the intellect, thereafter establish the mind in the *Atman*. It is the *Atman* which makes the whole mind luminous, and which makes it possible for you to know everything. The *Atman* is you, the consciousness. In the light of your consciousness the whole universe is lit, just like the dream world which not only exists in your consciousness, but is lit by it too. In the consciousness, the entire universe is being perceived by you. The mind and the intellect are all being perceived by you in the consciousness of the *Atman*. Thus having known, establish or fix your mind, in the Self, the *Atman*. Establish your awareness in the *Atman* with a mind which has undergone spiritual regeneration.

There are two words here, *atmaanam* and *atmana*. In the Bhagavad Gita, the word *atma* at times refers to the body, according to the context. Somtimes the word *atma* refers to the mind. Sometimes the word *atma* refers to the intellect. At times the word *atma* refers to the *jivatma*, the individual soul. At some places the word *atma*, according to the context also refers to *Atman*, the true Self.

So here are two words used, both as *atma*. The first word *atmaanam* refers to the mind. The second word *atmana* stands for the intellect. The intellect having appreciated and decided that the *Atman* is and exists everywhere. In its nature of being it is all pervasive, and everywhere, because it is its nature to be so. Thus your *Atman*, is the all-pervasive Divine. That is why it is said, God is everywhere. In the Godly state of existence, God exists everywhere. Since God exists everywhere, it naturally has to exist within you and outside you. With reference to this body, it exists within you, and with reference to the same body, outside you too.

So if it is there within you, it must be you. You cannot but be that, because it is there within you. Therefore, God-realization is called Self-realization. Once you realize God within you, at the same time, you would realize God everywhere, because it is everywhere. Thus that all-pervasive universal experience transpires. Therefore, since God is within you, it is you, and that is your essential nature. So the intellect has to appreciate God's beingness as the Self and establish the mind therein. By the intellect, (*atmana*) the mind (*atmaanam*) is fixed, or established in the Self, the *Atman*.

It is said that the *Atman* has no form, it is formless. It is of the same nature everywhere. It has no parts, and is unthinkable. The *Atman* cannot be thought of. You can think of this or that, but you cannot think directly of the *Atman* because the *Atman* has no form. It is neither gross nor subtle. It has no worldly or material characteristics and attributes. Therefore, the only way to fix your mind in the *Atman* is to quietly and silently be aware of it. That is all. The *Atman* being everywhere, one cannot particularly say the *Atman* is here, and is not there. All that you have to do is, with the decided intellect, fix the mind and establish it in the *Atman*, which is everywhere. Being so aware of the *Atman* is the quintessence of religion. That means you become silently aware of the *Atman* which is everywhere. It is subtle and imperceptible, but nevertheless, it exists everywhere. Therefore, you silently go about your life being aware of it. Thus you become aware of your beingness the *Atman*. Become consciously aware of the indwelling Self. That is all that you have to do. Just be aware of awareness, and this is meditation.

In meditation you are now trying to be aware or conscious of the Divine. What were you aware of before? You were aware of the world and things of the world. When you become aware of the world and the things of the world, you have lost your awareness of the *Atman*, which is subtle and imperceptible and everywhere. The only way to be aware of this *Atman* is to become silent, forget the world, and be aware of awareness. Thus there is nothing particular to focus your attention upon. There is no concentration here. It is only tp be aware. Keeping quiet, silently be aware. Once you become quiet, you have become dead to the world and to the thought world around you. Thus you become dead to the desire world too. And then, quietly maintain this awareness. Maintain vigil. This is how to be established in the *Atman*.

In the Katho Upanishad it is mentioned:

****

Yada panchavtistante jnanani manasa saha|
Buddhisca na vichestati tamahuhu paramam gatim||

When the mind along with its five sense organs of knowledge withdraws from its activities, and the intellect too remains quiescent (quiet), then that is said to be the supreme final state (of enlightened beingness.)
****

The five organs of knowledge along with the mind remain quiet and the intellect remains still. The mind does not oscillate into thought patterns and the five sense organs have been withdrawn from their sense perceptual functions. *Buddhi*, the intellect also does not undergo any movement. Then at that stage it is said, *paramaam gatim*. One abides in one's ineffable Divine state. At that point, you have established yourself in the ultimate reality, the final truth of life.

When you are in a state of silence you become acutely conscious or aware of awareness itself. Maintain this. As you keep on maintaining it, you become more and more intensely aware of the awareness, and then gradually you become absorbed in it. When you become more and more absorbed in it, then you reach the point wherein total absorption comes in. Thus when you get totally absorbed that is called *samaadhi*. The word *samaadhi* means the mystic state of inner communion. The mind is now established in the *Atman*.

When you go about functioning in the world, you still can maintain that awareness, and can silently function in all your activities. You become silently aware. The word is *smriti*. You have a recollection, a remembrance. You are to maintain that recollection in a very subtle way, and then go about doing your functions. When you are able to do that, then that is said to be living in God, or you are maintaining God-consciousness, or God-awareness.

Thus in this manner, when you are able to do this, Krishna says, there are two things accomplished. One is to be established in the *Atman*, and secondly to overcome its great impediment called desire. By that you are able to overcome *kaama* (desire). By this you are able to get it out of your system. This is the technique or method the Lord gives you to abide in the *Atman* and thus be enlightened to the reality of your true being.

Then when you are able to live your life in this manner, as a *karma yogin*, you will get gradually established in the *Atman*. This particular chapter is called as *karma yoga*. Recollect in your mind, and then try to live in your life, the science of *karma yoga*. At the same time, while performing your *karmas* also maintain the awareness of the *Atman*. When you are able to do this you are living in God-awareness. And this, in course of time will bring about God-realization, that is Self-realization.